Waterloo

Waterloo

by Commandant Henry Lachouque
Visual conception by Juan Carlos Carmigniani
Uniform plates by Baron Louis de Beaufort
Maps by Jean-Claude Quennevat

Introduction by David G. Chandler

ARMS AND ARMOUR PRESS

Published by Arms and Armour Press, Lionel Leventhal Limited, 2 – 6 Hampstead High Street, London NW3 1PR.

Printed in Great Britain by Cox & Wyman Limited, Fakenham.

SBN 85368 340 9

Acknowledgments

A portrait of Waterloo could be achieved only through the collaboration of all those in the world who attach importance to recreating a pictorial image of the exceptional grandeur of that moment in history. I therefore owe my warmest thanks to all those who were good enough to assist me in this effort. In particular, I am grateful to:

M. Jean Tranie, who was most helpful in making available to me the archives in the valuable collection of his relative, Commandant Henry Lachouque.

To Vicomte Henri de Beaufort for opening up to me his library – that of an enthusiastic collector – and giving me access to unpublished works.

To the Amicale des Collectionneurs de Figurines Historiques du Centre Loir d'Orléans for giving me permission to reproduce plates from *Les Uniformes de Waterloo*.

To Dr. F. G. Hourtoule for authorising the reproduction of plates by J. Girbal from *Soldats et Uniformes du Ier Empire*.

To Madame J. Augé and Lt. Col. Garros for permission to use illustrations from *Le Champ de Bataille de Waterloo*.

To the administrators of the Musée du Panorama de Waterloo for having authorised the reproduction of sequences of the masterly depictions of the battle.

To Colonel Wemaere, Curator, Musée de l'Armée, Paris.

To Monsieur Lorette, Deputy-Curator, Musée Royal de l'Armée, Brussels.

To Monsieur Pierre d'Harville, representative of the Souvenir Napoleonien for Hainaut.

To Cyrile Charbault, whose photographic talents enabled me to make the first mock-up of the work.

To the Lord Chamberlain, who was good enough to entrust to me precious documents from the private collection of H.M. The Queen; to the Wellington Museum (Apsley House), London; the Sheffield City Art Gallery; the National Army Museum, London; the Temple Newsarm House; the British Museum; the Victoria and Albert Museum; the Royal Artillery; the Radio Times Hulton Picture Library; the Scottish United Services Museum; the Black Watch Museum; the Marquess of Anglesey; and Editions Larousse. And finally to Valérie de Lannurien, who was given the difficult task of reconstructing the puzzle into pages. It is to her charm and application that I owe the realisation of my dream in print.

J.C.C.

Picture Sources.
Anderson-Giraudon, 17. Bulloz, 88, 187, 193, B.B.C. Publications, 152, 198. Cuvelier, 70, 71, 71, 71. Cooper Library, 150. Cyrile Charbaut, 95, 143, 200. René Dazy, 191 Dr. W. H. Findlay, 100. Flammarion, 44. Giraudon, 12, 18. P. d'Harville, 11, 63, 67, 67, 68, 68, 69, 73, 84, 85, 86, 89, 97, 107, 116, 116, 129, 134, 138, 141, 155, 189. Larousse, 14, 16. Magnum Lessing, 97, 105, 181, 183, 195. Mallinus, 161, 162–163, 164–165, 166–167, 168–168, 170–171, 172. Musée de l'Emperi, 46, 47. Rigal, 45, 160. Robin Livio, 91. Tom Scott, 135. Trosset, 65, 74, 89, 93, 97, 97, 143, 155, 156, 158, 160, 182, 186, 188. Roger Viollet, 15, 17, 18, 47, 52, 82, 87, 104, 136, 136, 176, 177. The maps were prepared by Michel Pluvinage. Finally, we are indebted to Mr. Tranié for a number of important documents from the personal collection of Commandant Lachouque.

Contents

List of maps

Introduction

By David G. Chandler

Of all the campaigns and battles fought in modern history, none has attracted more attention from soldiers and scholars than the dramatic events that took place in Belgium between 15th and 19th June 1815; but writing about the battles and campaigns of earlier times is no easy task, nor is it one to be undertaken lightly. The basic facts are not always easy to discover; and when they are found, it often proves difficult to reconcile one with another. Every battle has unique nuances and shifts of mood as well as aspects of special military importance, and to miss the fluctuating atmosphere of doubt and confidence, of fear and elation, is often to misrepresent the true events, albeit unwittingly. These qualitative factors – which, besides states of morale, include standards of training, efficiency of weapons and equipment and, above all, the qualities of leadership displayed at every level of command – are often of greater significance than purely quantitative considerations. God may, on occasion, appear to favour "the big battalions", but military history is also full of significant contrary examples ranging from Marathon in the era before Christ, through such famous battles as Agincourt in 1415, to the Arab-Israeli conflict of 1967. The writer, therefore, in seeking to do justice to his subject, must attempt to qualify as well as quantify – and in this, considerations of personal inclination and national bias inevitably enter into the picture.

Although there has been no lack of interpreters of what transpired in 1815, it is noteworthy that only one of the three principal protagonists produced a first-hand account. Field-Marshal Blücher had no pretensions to scholarship; and the Duke of Wellington, who possessed considerable literary gifts – even if his style was, to modern eyes, somewhat stiff and patrician – deliberately chose not to reveal his thoughts on paper. This reticence was partly due to a degree of aloofness and a feeling that to write the true history of events so soon after the battle would lead to major distortions. Besides which, he was also aware that many fine reputations would never survive the harsh examination of scholarly investigation. "The history of a battle is not unlike the history of a ball," he wrote to one would-be historian of Waterloo, John Croker. "Some individuals may recollect all the little events of which the great result is the battle won or lost; but no individual can recollect the order in which, or the exact moment at which, they occurred, which makes all the difference to their value or importance Then the faults of the misbehaviour of some gave occasion for the distinction of others, and perhaps were the cause of material losses; and you cannot write a true history of a battle without including the faults and misbehaviour of part at least of those engaged. Believe me that every man you see in a military uniform is not a hero . . ." On a later occasion the Duke was even more scathing about pen-pushers, remarking that he was ". . . really disgusted with and ashamed of all that I have seen (read) of the battle. The number of writings upon it would lead the world to believe that the British Army had never fought a battle before." Fortunately for posterity, however, the Duke was not averse to dropping, in passing, many useful comments and remarks that were assiduously noted by his interlocutors; but the fact remains that he never produced, even verbally, a comprehensive account.

No such reticence distinguished the third commander-in-chief, the Emperor Napoleon. Part of the long years of exile at Longwood on St. Helena were devoted to dictating his memoirs to Baron Gourgaud and other members of his small entourage. For this, posterity may be grateful; but great care has to be exercised in judging Napoleon's recollections of past events. It would be positively dangerous to place undue reliance on his accuracy. Napoleon was never noted for his modesty and the main purpose of the parts of the *Relations of St. Helena* referring to the campaign of 1815 was to produce a polemical self-exculpatory vindication of what had transpired. Determined to propagate the legend that his fall had been that of a giant encompassed by pygmies, he did not hesitate to ascribe the outcome to the crass errors of Marshal Ney and Marshal Grouchy, in the latter case going so far as to make accusations of treason and treachery. But as Commandant Lachouque makes quite clear in this book, Napoleon himself was in a large measure the author of his own misfortunes. The ultimate responsibility – whether for victory or defeat – inevitably lies on the shoulders of the commander-in-chief.

If not much of direct value was forthcoming from the principal actors at Waterloo, there was a plethora of information from the myriad members of the supporting cast of all nations – only serving to compound the confusion. Throughout the nineteenth century there was a veritable flood of memoirs written by soldiers of every rank whose recollections, however softened or distorted by the passage of the years, were avidly snatched up by publishers quick to appreciate the profits that could be made from exploiting the intense popular interest in the history of Waterloo. Wellington's scornful remark already cited referred to the outpourings of fact intermixed with a liberal dosage of fiction that poured from the presses in his own lifetime.

Naturally, different authors interpret the basic events of 1815 from their own highly individualistic viewpoints. But this is no fault. A clear point of view is, indeed, a vital ingredient for any work of military history, for this is what gives a book life and purpose. On the other hand, a work of historical value must not be devoted to sensationalism or distortion of the facts. A balance has to be struck, therefore, between conflicting claims and concepts – but within that balance, a considerable variation of national sentiments and special interpretations may be fairly entertained and expressed. This present volume is a case in point. The late Commandant Henri Lachouque was a French writer of great repute in the Napoleonic field. Throughout a long career he produced over twenty volumes on military aspects of the Napoleonic period, no less than three of which were devoted to the subject of Waterloo: *Le Secret de Waterloo, Waterloo: Guide illustré* and *Waterloo: La fin d'un monde.* He was thus no stranger to the subject. Probably his best known and most celebrated work was *Napoléon et la Garde Imperiale* (published in English as *The Anatomy of Glory*), which was a monument of scholarship and was probably his chef d'oeuvre.

The sampling of a few pages of this translation of *Waterloo* will convince the reader that Henry Lachouque was, not unexpectedly, an extreme chauvinist – a romantic, wholly devoted to the sentiments of "la gloire"; the cherisher of the memory of France's Napoleonic armies. Serious students might regret that the author, confident in his scholarship, did not see fit to reveal his sources or produce references – signposts that would have proved invaluable in following up some of the good Commandant's most controversial claims. But no reader will fail to admire the pace and vivacity of his writing style, which the translators have managed to capture to a remarkable degree. This, then, is a volume that will present a knowledgeable reader with much enjoyment, many challenging ideas and, quite probably (for all but the most extreme Napoleon worshipper), no little exasperation from time to time. Nevertheless, none can deny this book's extreme readability or the author's flair for making the most prosaic facts and figures appear dramatically alive. Some will feel that certain of his claims and interpretations are close to the limit of historical credibility – and one or two of them beyond that boundary – but this makes for some intriguing reading.

Most studies of this brief campaign break down into four main chronological sections, and Commandant Lachouque has followed the convention. First, the strategic background that led to the fresh outbreak of hostilities is sketched in, together with basic information about the commanders and their armies. Next, the opening events are given attention – the launching of the French offensive over the Sambre and the Allied and Prussian responses. Third, the opportunities made and lost, the early actions won, conceded or drawn and the fateful decisions on which the future of Europe probably depended receive careful and detailed consideration, together with the sequence of events leading up to the great crisis – the major engagement. And fourth, the great battle, with its six stages, shifts of fortune, errors of tactics and judgment, is carefully described and analysed. However contentious some of the assertions and conclusions, all of this will be found in the pages that follow.

A good picture is worth many hundreds of words, and this sumptuous edition is

The return from the Isle of Elba. Painting by Steuben. Bibliothèque Nationale, Paris.

beautifully and comprehensively illustrated – one major reason for its production, as the Preface makes clear. The volume makes a superb visual impact, and this is one of its greatest strengths. It may be essentially a "drum and trumpet" saga that is unfolded within its pages, but it is a fine example of its type and many readers will find hours of enjoyment within its pages. "History is an argument without end" as Professor Geyl remarked, and that constitutes one of the subject's greatest charms. We may not agree with Commandant Lachouque's final sentiment – that it has taken Europe 150 years to restore the dream of international unity and cooperation that was destroyed at the battle of Waterloo – although it is sometimes quite clear that no small number of modern Frenchmen would applaud his view – but we may strongly defend his right to express it.

David G. Chandler
Royal Military Academy
Sandhurst

Preface

Far from obliterating the Waterloo legend, contemporary history has magnified its lesson tenfold. It is now evident that the fascination exerted by that tragedy has been enhanced by two world wars in which Europe was faced with problems of similar magnitude.

This fascination stems as much from the epic character of the drama, conceived as a predestined confrontation during one of the most fabulous epochs of modern history, as from the vital importance of the issues at stake. And one might well wonder whether the convulsions that have shaken Europe for over a century are not, in fact, the direct consequence or, perhaps, the historic reflection of Waterloo.

Each instant of those four days, and the motive underlying each of them, has been analysed in hundreds of books without finally settling the argument. But the story of Waterloo has not only been told by historians, poets and philosophers: it has also been portrayed in pictures.

This portrait of the battle is at once so rich, so beautiful and so varied that it can be advantageously compared with the first-hand accounts, filmed and broadcast, that so vividly depicted the day-by-day events of the Second World War, Innumerable sketching-artists and painters, famous and unknown, from the five countries concerned in the battle have been inspired to pay homage to the heroism and nobility of the adversaries who surpassed themselves on that day of mortal conflict.

The cinema naturally seized on the theme and, from the silent films to the latest super-productions, has always treated it in epic style.

A researcher and collector of statuettes and documents dealing with the Napoleonic era, I have been haunted since childhood by the drama of Waterloo and have eagerly searched for all the illustrated material I could find to recreate the battle. I believe the time has now come to make this old dream come true by grouping, collating and selecting this material to transform the history of legend and invest it with what might be called an aesthetic dimension, at once more human and more authentic: a kind of film from these impressions of the 1815 campaign.

This would not have been possible without a great deal of friendly and considerate collaboration. Baron Louis de Beaufort's talent for military illustration and his thorough knowledge of the uniforms, insignia and colours of the Grand Armée are well known. I would like to thank him here for devoting his talent, at my request, to the painting of his admirable series of uniforms worn by the belligerents at Waterloo.

I am also grateful to Jean-Claude Quennevat, author of *L'Atlas de la Grande Armée* and *Les Vrais soldats de Napoléon,* for kindly adjusting his map-making gifts to the perspectives of this work. Nothing would have been achieved with such true historical conscientiousness, however, if I had not had the privilege not only of the advice but also of the invaluable friendship of the greatest military historian of the Empire – Commandant Henry Lachouque – who, before his death, expressed keen interest in my project. He personally gave me permission to make use of his masterly work *Napoléon à Waterloo,* which proved so well adapted to the original portrait I wanted to present.

By dint of much friendly help in search of essential texts, I have been able to assemble portraits, battle scenes, maps and landscapes signed by artists such as Knötel, Rocholl, Lady Butler, Dighton, Crofts, Woodville, Charretier, Chaperon, Detaille, Augé, Lalauze and others, in addition to the magnificent panorama of Waterloo by the painters Demoulin, Malespina, Desvarreux and Robiquet – the colour reproduction of which is unquestionably the most striking feature of this book.

The amalgamation of topography, history, uniforms and insignia herein has been carefully designed to enable the reader to form for himself a complete picture of the battle. The strict accuracy of the text and the accompanying illustrations make it possible to relive in minute detail what was to be Napoleon's last campaign.

J.C.C.

1. Europe against Napoleon

Napoleon in 1815.
Lithograph by Horace Vernet. In 1815 he was still the greatest of the contemporary military leaders. Never before had he taken command so effectively; but because his orders were misunderstood and therefore poorly executed the result was the failure of one of his most brilliant strategic concepts. "I felt that I was running out of luck. I was no longer convinced of ultimate success," he declared at St. Helena, "and if one is not prepared to take risks when the time is ripe, one ends up by doing nothing – and of course, one should never take a risk without being sure that one will be lucky."

Europe at the Congress of Vienna

A drama in four acts, with a prologue.

The prologue lasted twenty-three years; the drama lasted four days. On 20th April 1792 the French Republic declared war on Europe. Bonaparte won the war and made peace (1802). Then came revenge, followed by rescue operations. On the prongs of Neptune's trident, and at a cost of £54,000,000 sterling, Napoleon fell (1814).

On 1st March 1815, while the Congress of Vienna was attempting to redraw the map of Europe, Napoleon rose again – or was resurrected. On 13th March the Emperor was declared by the Allies to be beyond the protection of international law, and on 20th March he was in Paris. On 25th March the Coalition – spurred on by fear, hate and £5,000,000 sterling – had been reconstituted. Objective: the defeat of Napoleon and the dismemberment of France. Means: England, Russia, Austria and Prussia binding themselves to "keep 150,000 men constantly in the field, of which 15,000 would be cavalry, and employ them actively against the common enemy".

"I place the utmost importance on preserving the peace with your Majesty," ventured the Emperor in a letter of 1st April addressed to each sovereign.

A futile profession of faith . . . War was inevitable. It was therefore necessary to prepare for it.

Congress of Vienna. Water-colour sketch by Jean Baptiste Isabey.

Congress of Vienna. *Painting by Jean Baptiste Isabey.* Standing from left to right: *Duke of Wellington (Britain); Count de Lobo (Portugal); Count Saldanha (Portugal); von Löwenhielm (Sweden); Count of Noailles (France); Prince von Metternich (Austria); Latour du Pin (France); leaning on chair, Count Nesselrode (Russia); behind chair, Dalberg (France); Prince Razumovsky (Russia); Lord Stewart (Britain); Earl of Clancarty (Britain); Wacken (Prussia); Chevalier von Gentz (Austria); Baron von Humboldt (Prussia); Earl Cathcart (Britain).* Sitting from left to right: *Prince von Hardenberg (Prussia); Count de Palmella (Portugal); Viscount Castlereagh (Britain); Baron Wessenberg (Austria); Count de Labrador (Spain); Prince de Talleyrand (France); Count Stackelberg (Russia).*

When the Treaty of Paris was signed, on 30th May 1814, the coalition powers decided to hold the Congress of Vienna to settle the distribution of the territories formerly occupied by or allied to France. The France of Louis XVIII had been granted representation but without power to participate in discussions. The 'Big Four' among the conquerors – Russia, Austria, Prussia and Great Britain – having reserved all rights, found negotiations in respect of the fate of Poland, Saxony and the Rhineland particularly difficult since these territories were claimed by both Russia and Prussia. These territorial claims caused concern in England and Austria. Talleyrand, representing France, took advantage of the dissensions and entered into a secret treaty of alliance with England and Austria that restored to France her position among the great powers.

Since his departure from Elba, Napoleon had tried to convince the Congress of Vienna that his intentions were peaceful. The reply to his overtures was contained in the Declaration of 13th March, which named "the Corscian adventurer, by a proclamation of Europe, as a public enemy and a threat to the world".

By a Treaty of 29th June 1814, renewed on 25th March 1815, the four great powers pledged themselves to keep a force of 150,000 men under arms "until such time as Bonaparte will have been rendered absolutely incapable of causing further trouble by renewing his attempts to seize supreme power in France and threatening the safety of Europe". Under a special provision, it was agreed that Great Britain would pay a cash subsidy to compensate for her numerically inferior contingent.

13

Alexander I, Emperor of Russia. *By François Pascal Simon, Baron Gérard. Apsley House.*

Count von Nesselrode. *Engraving by Hoffmeister. Bibliothèque Nationale, Paris.*

Alexander I, 1777–1825. Son of Paul I, Alexander was the most powerful sovereign in Europe and was apparently fascinated by the personality of Napoleon. Russian ambitions in the Orient and in Europe constantly clashed with those of the French Empire, leading to the conflict of 1812 and Napoleon's subsequent abdication. Becoming Supreme Commander of the Allied armies in 1814, Alexander was popular in France and helped to keep the Allied claims in check at the Congress of Vienna. He became Napoleon's most relentless enemy during the Hundred Days.

Count von Nesselrode, 1780–1862. Russian diplomat, attaché at the Russian Embassy in Paris from 1808 to 1811. In 1813 he urged Alexander I to continue the war against France. He was the Russian delegate to the Congress of Vienna.

Prince von Metternich. *Lithograph by C. Constans, after Lieder. Bibliothèque Nationale, Paris.*

Francis I, Emperor of Austria, 1768–1835. *By Anton Einsle. Apsley House.*

Prince von Metternich was Austria's ambassador in Paris from 1808 to 1809. He then became Minister for Foreign Affairs of Austria, and Chancellor in 1809. He arranged the marriage between Marie-Louise and Napoleon and concluded a treaty of alliance with France. After the Russian campaign, he prepared a revenge that resulted in Austria joining the Coalition in 1813.

Francis I, first hereditary sovereign of Austria, was the last German Emperor of the Holy Roman Empire, dissolved following the establishment of the Confederation of the Rhine in 1806. At the time of the Congress of Vienna, he was President of the Germanic Confederation. Although he was Napoleon's father-in-law, as a convinced monarchist he considered his son-in-law the personification of the French Revolution – someone who had to be destroyed in order to restore the legitimate succession to France.

During the French invasion of 1807 John VI fled to Brazil, where he was still living in exile in 1815. He was represented at the Congress of Vienna by the Count of Palmella, the delegate of the Portuguese Regency Council.

John VI, King of Portugal, 1769–1826. Artist unknown. Apsley House.

Frederick-William III, King of Prussia, 1770–1840. *Artist unknown. Apsley House.*

Frederick William, grand-nephew of Frederick the Great, was married to Louise of Prussia, whose beauty and patriotism are legendary. After the defeat by the French in 1806, which deprived Prussia of half of its former territories, he became Napoleon's most implacable enemy. Under his leadership, Prussia became an eager participant in the War of Liberation of 1813 and 1814.

Prince von Hardenberg was forced by Napoleon to resign his post as Prussia's Minister for Foreign Affairs after the Treaty of Tilsit. Chancellor in 1810, he became one of the architects of the reconstruction of Prussia. He represented his sovereign at the Congress of Vienna, where he strove to obtain the dismemberment of France.

Prince von Hardenberg, 1750–1822.

16

Ferdinand VII, King of Spain, 1784–1833. By Goya. Prado Museum.

In 1808 the Prince of the Asturias became Ferdinand VII, King of Spain, following the Aranjuez riots. He was later forced to abdicate during an interview with Napoleon at Bayonne, was made prisoner at Valençay, but regained his throne in 1814. He was represented at the Congress of Vienna by the Chevalier de Labrador. After participating in the Declaration of 13th March, he appealed to his subjects to enter the war "in the name of justice, humanity and religion".

George IV, Prince Regent, 1762–1830. By Sir David Wilkie. Apsley House.

The Prince Regent – more interested in his private life than in matters of State – gave control to his ministers, who acted without magnanimity when Napoleon "placed himself under the protection of the British people".

Viscount Castlereagh, Marquis of Londonderry, Foreign Secretary in 1812, created the Coalition that was to defeat Napoleon. He was responsible for the Treaty of Chaumont in 1814. Plenipotentiary at the Congress of Vienna, he was in favour of a balance of power; and his influence was decisive during the drawing up of the two Treaties of Paris that restored France's former boundaries in 1814 and prevented her dismemberment in 1815.

Viscount Castlereagh, Marquis of Londonderry, 1768–1822. Minister Plenipotentiary.

17

Louis XVIII, King of France, 1755–1824. *By Baron Antoine Jean Gros. Collection of the Duke of Treviso.*

Twenty years of exile did not change his concern for the augustness of royalty. King by divine right, he resigned himself to the constitutional Charter dating back to the nineteenth year of his reign – but without ever approving it. A refugee in Ghent during the Hundred Days, he supported the Allies in their fight against Napoleon.

Prince de Talleyrand Perigord, 1754–1838. *Painting by Mlle. Godefroy (detail).*

Minister of Foreign Affairs for France from 1797, formerly Bishop of Autun, then Prince of Benevento in 1806 and finally Prince de Talleyrand in 1814, he was to take part in all the governments that he first set up and then, in turn, disowned. After the disfavour he earned during the meeting between Napoleon and Alexander at Erfurt in 1808, he nevertheless remained one of the French Empire's leading dignitaries. As the principal architect of the restoration of the Bourbons, he represented France at the Congress of Vienna where, as a result of the dissensions among the Allies, he managed to obtain the recognition of France as a great power.

The military situation in Europe, May 1815

After the escaped prisoner from the Isle of Elba had been proclaimed an outlaw on 13th March, almost 800,000 men threatened the French frontiers, including an Anglo-Spanish corps on the frontier of the Pyrenees.

Napoleon had at his disposal a striking force of only 125,000 fighting men. Because of the enormous imbalance of the forces face to face, and on the assumption that the Coalition army would not march on Paris before 15th July, the Emperor decided to forestall the invasion of France by himself launching an attack on Belgium. He hoped that in fighting Wellington and Blücher separately, before they had time to join forces, their defeat would result in the liberation of a large part of Belgium and the fall of the British Government.

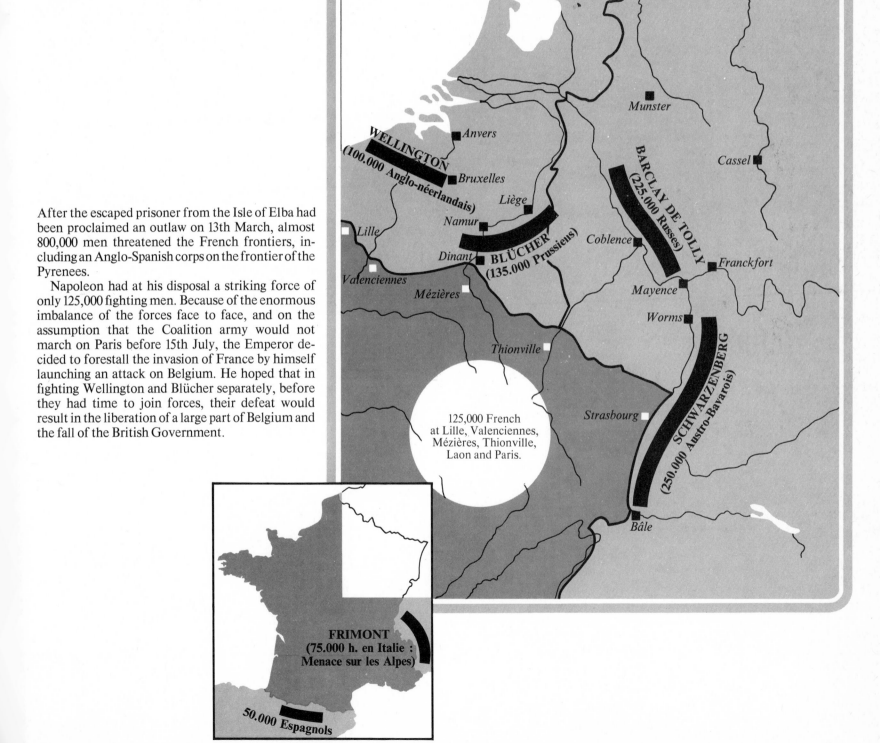

WELLINGTON
(100.000 Anglo-néerlandais)

BLÜCHER
(135.000 Prussiens)

BARCLAY DE TOLLY
(225.000 Russes)

SCHWARZENBERG
(250.000 Austro-Bavarois)

125,000 French
at Lille, Valenciennes,
Mézières, Thionville,
Laon and Paris.

Munster
Anvers
Bruxelles
Liège
Namur
Lille
Dinant
Valenciennes
Mézières
Coblence
Mayence
Worms
Thionville
Strasbourg
Cassel
Franckfort
Bâle

FRIMONT
(75.000 h. en Italie :
Menace sur les Alpes)

50.000 Espagnols

2. Armed forces in the field

Sir Arthur Wellesley, Field-Marshal the Duke of Wellington, 1769–1852. *Drawing by Denis Dighton. The Royal Library, Windsor. Reproduced by the gracious permission of H.M. the Queen.*

Sir Arthur Wellesley was the same age as Napoleon. After distinguishing himself in India and in the Peninsular War, he was created Duke of Wellington. In attendance at the Congress of Vienna at the time of Napoleon's return, he was given command of the Army of the Low Countries, which was assembled in Belgium. Well supported by his generals, he held Ney in check at Quatre-Bras and resisted Napoleon at Waterloo until the Prussians arrived.

The coalition that had conducted the 1814 campaign was still under arms. Four marching orders, issued in Vienna, sufficed to send the armies of Prussia, Austria, Germany and Russia to the frontiers; 50,000 Anglo-Hanoverians were stationed in Holland. Five armies of first-line troops were formed.

Two of these mustered in Belgium. One was the Army of the Low Countries and the other was the Army of the Lower Rhine.

The Army of the Low Countries consisted of English, Scottish and Irish troops, German mercenaries, Dutch and Belgians under the orders of the "Conqueror of the Peninsula", the Duke of Wellington, who had his headquarters in Brussels. This army kept watch on the French frontier extending from the North Sea to Mons. Its supply centre was Ostend.

It was made up of two army corps, the first under the Prince of Orange, consisting of four divisions – 30,000 men – surrounding Ath. The second, under Lord Hill, consisted of three and a half divisions – 24,000 men – at Nivelles, Braine-le-Comte, Enghien. Infantry reserves totalled 25,000 men under orders from the Duke in Brussels. Cavalry reserves, under Lord Uxbridge, were 11,000 men at Grammont. In all, there were 83,000 men and 210 guns.

It was an incongruous army. The component units had nothing in common – neither language nor ideas, neither customs nor canons. It was an army of mercenaries based on Dutch recruits and militiamen with a few Belgians thrown in, known as the Netherlands Army; tough British regulars who never tired; foot soldiers described by Wellington as "the scum of the earth, enlisted for drink" but unflinching in defence and good in musketry, drilled without mercy by non-commissioned officers who were martinets, led by officers who were stand-offish, young, often inexperienced, but brave – gentlemen rather than soldiers. The cavalry was bold, well-mounted and imbued with the traditional spirit

The Army of the Low Countries

of sacrifice. The artillery was weak and badly officered. It was a branch of service less popular than the others because it was "really too scholarly". Generals Colin Halkett, F. Adam, J. Kempt and D. Pack were tough and brave commanders; Sir Thomas Picton, who had seen Colonial service, was a hero of the Spanish War and was known for his character, tenacity and gallantry. The cavalry generals Sir William Ponsonby, Lord Edward Somerset, Sir Colquhoun Grant and Sir John Vandeleur had been soundly initiated in the art of warfare in Spain.

The mercenaries of the King's German Legion – undisciplined Saxons and heavily-built Hanoverians who took discipline seriously – were under the command of Lieutenant-General Sir Charles Alten and Major-General Sir William Dörnberg, among others.

The Dutch – ponderous, solid – were under the command of young William Frederick George Louis, hereditary Prince of Orange and Nassau, who was 23 years old. He had served on Wellington's staff in Spain. Cordial, well-liked, madly brave, he was no army general; but his Chief of Staff, Major-General de Constant-Rebecque, who had formerly been an officer in Louis XVI's Swiss Guards and had escaped the massacre in the Tuileries on 10th August 1792 – a Dutch officer at Fleurus, a Prussian officer at Auerstädt, an English officer in Spain – was one of the military geniuses of his time. Under their command were General Perponcher-Sedlnitzky – a veteran of the Egyptian campaign, on the side of the English; Chassé; Collaert; van Merlen; Trip van Soudtlant; and van Chigny, who had served for some time in the French Army.

Right: Lieutenant-General Sir Thomas Picton, 1758–1815, killed on 18th June at the beginning of the battle. By Sir William Beechey. Apsley House. Charged with the command of the left flank of the Army of the Low Countries, he was killed at the beginning of the battle in leading the counterattack by Kempt's brigade against the French 1st Corps. He had taken the field in civilian clothes, having rejoined the army without his baggage.

Lord Uxbridge, Marquis of Anglesey, 1768–1854, commander of the cavalry corps of the Army of the Low Countries. One of the last cannon shots by the French artillery on 18th June severed his right leg. By Jan Willem Pieneman. Apsley House.

Lieutenant-General Lord Hill, 1772–1842, commander of the 2nd Corps of the Army of the Low Countries.

The General Staff was weak and badly recruited. "The pedants of High Wycombe are the ruin of the army," wrote Wellington.

Judging from paintings of episodes in the campaign, the army uniforms had many a touch of fantasy. The overall impression is of a rather highly-coloured picture by Epinal; but in point of fact it was a somewhat sorry mixture and, from the standpoint of military efficiency, a mediocre and strange combination of units consisting of highly-trained men and raw recruits coming from five different countries and speaking four different languages.

Its leader – Arthur Wellesley, Duke of Wellington, Irish, 46 years old – was a good organiser, an astute tactician, dictatorial, prudent, tenacious: "the Iron Duke". Fastidious in his personal habits (he shaved twice a day), he toured the billets speaking to the soldiers, seldom uttering a word of congratulation but maintaining the slightly cynical, caustic humour that was peculiar to him. "I have an infamous army, very weak, ill-equipped, motley," he wrote. Perhaps . . . but he knew very well how to handle it; and he repeated modestly, "I'll do the best I can . . ."

John Fremantle, aide-de-camp to Wellington. By Jan Willem Pieneman. Apsley House.

Lieutenant-Colonel Lord Fitzroy Somerset, 1788–1855, became Lord Raglan in 1852. He was to become commander of the British Expeditionary Force in the Crimea. Attached to Wellington's staff, he lost his right arm at Waterloo. By Jan Willem Pieneman. Apsley House.

Major-General Sir Denis Pack, commander of the British 9th Brigade (Picton's division). After a painting by Sanders.

Lieutenant-General Sir Charles Colville, commander of the Anglo-Hanoverian 4th Division of the Army of the Low Countries. By Sir Henry Raeburn.

The army of the Low Countries~Organisation

Commander-in-Chief: Field-Marshal the Duke of Wellington.

Military Secretary: Lieutenant-Colonel Lord Fitzroy Somerset. 8 Aides-de-camp.

Quartermaster-General: Colonel Sir W. de Lancey.

Commander, Artillery: Colonel Sir G. A. Wood.

Commander, Engineers: Lieutenant-Colonel Carmichael Smyth.

Commander-in-Chief of the Anglo-Hanoverian troops and of the King's German Legion: Lieutenant-General Count Alten.

Commander-in-Chief of the Netherlands troops and of the 1st Corps: Prince William of Orange.
6 English Senior Staff Officers.
8 Netherlands Senior Staff Officers.

Assistant Adjutant-General, British troops: Lieutenant-Colonel Sir G. H. Berkeley.

Chief of Staff, Netherlands troops: Major-General J. V. de Constant-Rebecque.

Commander-in-Chief 2nd Corps: Lieutenant-General Lord Hill.

I Corps

British 1st Division: Major-General George Cooke.
  1st Brigade: Major-General P. Maitland
  2nd Brigade: Major-General John Byng   4,000
  2 batteries
British 2nd Division: Lieutenant-General Count Alten.
  British 5th Brigade: Major-General Sir Colin
    Halkett   2,000
  King's German Legion 2nd Brigade:
    Colonel Ompteda   1,800
Hanoverian 1st Brigade: Major-General Count
  von Kielmansegge
2 batteries   3,000
                                                ─────
                                                7,550

23

Netherlands 2nd Division: Lieutenant-General Baron de Perponcher-Sedlnitzky.

- 1st Brigade: Major-General van Bijlandt — 2.7 — 3,200
- 2nd Brigade: Prince Bernard of Saxe-Weimar — 3.9 — 4,370
- 2 batteries ••

7,770

Netherlands 3rd Division: Lieutenant-General Chassé.

- 1st Brigade: Colonel Detmers — 2.6 — 3,000
- 2nd Brigade: Major-General d'Aubremé — 3.4 — 3,500
- 2 batteries ••

7,000

Netherlands Cavalry Division: Lieutenant-General de Collaërt.

- Brigade of Carabiniers: Major-General Trip van Zoutelande — 1.2 — 1,200
- 1st Brigade of Light Cavalry: Major-General de Ghigny — 1.0 — 1,000
- 2nd Brigade of Light Cavalry: Major-General van Merlen — 1.0 — 1,000
- 3 batteries ••

3,400

Total: 25,000 men and 66 artillery pieces.

II Corps

British 2nd Division: Lieutenant-General Sir Henry Clinton.

- British 3rd Brigade: Major-General F. Adam — 2.5 — 2,600
- King's German Legion, 1st Brigade: Lieutenant-Colonel G. C. A. du Plat — 1.7 — 2,000
- Hanoverian 3rd Brigade: Colonel H. Halkett — 2.4 — 2,500
- 2 batteries ••

7,600

British 4th Division: Lieutenant-General Sir Charles Colville.

- British 4th Brigade: Colonel H. Mitchell — 1.8 — 1,700
- British 6th Brigade: Major-General G. Johnstone — 2,500
- Hanoverian 6th Brigade: Major-General Sir J. Lyon — 3,000
- 2 batteries •

7,700

Netherlands Army Division: Prince Frederick of the Netherlands.

Netherlands 1st Division: Lieutenant-General J. A. Stedman — 3,400

- 1st Brigade: Major-General D'Hauw — 3,000
- 2nd Brigade: Major-General De Eerens — 3,000
- 1 battery

9,800

Total: 23,700 men and 66 artillery pieces.

The Reserve

British 5th Division: Lieutenant-General Sir Thomas Picton.

- British 8th Brigade: Major-General Sir J. Kempt — 2.0 — 2,400
- Hanoverian 5th Brigade: Colonel von Vincke — 2.4 — 2,500
- British 9th Brigade: Major-General Sir Denis Pack — 1.6 — 2,000
- 2 batteries •

7,000

British 6th Division: Lieutenant-General Sir L. Cole.

- British 10th Brigade: Major-General Sir J. Lambert — 2.1 — 2,500
- Hanoverian 4th Brigade: Colonel C. Best — 2.4 — 2,500
- 2 batteries •

5,000

Nassau Contingent: Major-General von Kruse

- 1st Duke of Nassau Regiment: Colonel de Steuben — 2.4 — 2,900

Brunswick Corps: H.S.H. Frederick William, Duke of Brunswick — 4.6 — 5,800

British Artillery Reserve: Major P. Drummond.

- 5 batteries ••••• — 1,400

Total: 30,000 men and 66 artillery pieces.

Anglo-German Cavalry

Commander-in-Chief: Lieutenant-General the Earl of Uxbridge.

- Household Brigade: Major-General Lord Edward Somerset — 1.2 — 1,200
- 2nd Brigade: Major-General Sir W. Ponsonby — 1.2 — 1,100
- 3rd Brigade: Major-General Sir W. Dörnberg — 1.2 — 1,400
- 4th Brigade: Major-General Sir J. Vandeleur — 1.2 — 1,100
- 5th Brigade: Major-General Sir C. Grant — 1.2 — 1,400
- 6th Brigade: Major-General Sir H. Vivian — 1.2 — 1,300
- 7th Brigade: Colonel F. Arentschildt — 1.2 — 1,400
- Hanoverian 1st Brigade: Colonel von Estorff — 1,600
- 6 batteries ✓

10,500

OVERALL TOTAL: 70,000 FOOT, 15,000 HORSE AND 219 GUNS.

1st Foot Guards. Regimental Colour.

The British

71st (Highland) Light Infantry.

1, sergeant; 2, piper; 3, corporal; 4, company officer in field dress; 5, bugler in field dress; 6, field officer; 7, soldier in field dress; 8a, company officer's jacket; 8b, detail of bugle-horn on turn-back; 9a, officer's shako; 9b, detail of badge on officer's shako; 10, shoulder-belt plate; 11, soldier's shako (private or non-commissioned officer); 12, musician's jacket; 13, bugle (model prior to 1812 but probably carried at Waterloo). This is one of the most famous of Scottish regiments. Changed into a light infantry regiment in 1809, it still retained several details of its Scottish uniform.

1st Regiment of Foot Guards.

1, sergeant, light company; 2, ensign, light company; 3, soldier, grenadier company; 4, ensign with colour; 5, bugler, light company; 6, pioneer; 7a, shako plate (brass for soldiers and gilt and enamel for officers) with the garter, star and royal cipher on red ground; 7b, valise badge of brass; 7c, shoulder-belt plate; 8, epaulette of an officer of a centre company; 9, officer's sword, flank companies; 10, wing of company officer of the light company. The British Foot Guards consisted of three regiments: the 1st Foot Guards (Grenadier Guards); the 2nd Foot Guards (Coldstream Guards); the 3rd Foot Guards (Scots Guards). The light companies of the Foot Guards distinguished themselves in the defence of Hougoumont.

92nd Regiment of Foot.
Fragment of Regimental
Colour.

92nd (Highland) Regiment of Foot (Gordon Highlanders).
1, bandsman; 2, officer in field dress; 3, drum-major; 4, colour-sergeant, light company; 5, mounted field officer; 6, private, battalion company; 7, drummer; 8, officer's jacket; 9a, epaulette worn by Colonel Cameron; 9b, officer's shoulder-belt plate; 9c, grenadier company officer's wing; 10, soldier's shoulder-belt plate. The 92nd Regiment of Foot was one of three Scottish regiments to wear kilts at Waterloo. The other two were the 42nd (Black Watch) and the 79th (Cameron Highlanders).

The British

Fig Nº 6

Fig Nº 7

Fig Nº 8

Fig Nº 5

Fig Nº 9

Fig Nº 2

Fig Nº 3

Fig Nº 4

Luy de Beaufort

Fig Nº 1

Regiments of Heavy Cavalry.
1, officer, 1st King's Dragoon Guards; 2, trooper, 1st King's Dragoon Guards; 3, corporal, 1st (Royal) Dragoons; 4, trumpeter, 1st (Royal) Dragoons; 5, officer's jacket, 1st King's Dragoon Guards; 6, pouch with carbine belt; 7, heavy cavalry helmet; 8, dragoon's sword; 9, officer's jacket, 1st (Royal) Dragoons.

Fig nº6

Fig nº7

Fig nº8

Fig nº9

Fig nº10

Fig nº11

Fig nº1

Fig nº2

Fig nº3

Fig nº5

Fig nº4

2nd Royal North British Dragoons (Scots Greys).
1, sergeant in field dress; 2, trumpeter in field dress; 3, private in field dress; 4, officer; 5, officer in field dress; 6, officer's lace, detail; 7, officer's sword; 8, officer's jacket; 9, private's bearskin cap; 10, saddle and valise; 11, waist-belt clasp. Although its official name was the 2nd Royal North British Dragoons, this regiment was later better known as the Scots Greys – the name deriving from the colour of the horses. At Waterloo it formed part of the 2nd Cavalry Brigade.

The Light Dragoons.
1, private of the 13th Light Dragoons in field dress; 2, officer of the 12th Prince of Wales's Light Dragoons; 3, private of the 11th Light Dragoons; 4, officer of the 16th Light Dragoons; 5, private of the 12th Light Dragoons; 6, officer of the 13th Light Dragoons; 7, trumpeter of the 11th Light Dragoons; 8, private's shako; 9, officer's jacket; 10, private's saddle and valise; 11, officer's sabretache, 12th Light Dragoons; 12, officer's shako.

The Royal Horse Artillery.
1, field officer; 2, sergeant; 3, trumpeter; 4, gunner of the Mounted Rocket Corps; 5, gunner; 6, gunner (back view); 7, detail of gunner's jacket; 8, helmet (the same basic design was used for officers and gunners); 9, officer's jacket, cuff detail. The Royal Horse Artillery was created in 1793. In 1815 a Horse Artillery troop consisted of five officers (including a surgeon), 187 sergeants, corporals, trumpeters, gunners and drivers, with five guns, one howitzer, 13 waggons of different sorts, and 226 horses and mules.

The British

The forces of the United Netherlands

Nassau. Colour of the 2nd Regiment of Light Infantry.

William, Prince of Orange Nassau, *future King of Holland, 1792–1848. Netherlands Army Museum, Perthuislaan, Leiden. He served under the Duke of Wellington in Spain from 1811. Commander-in-Chief of the Netherlands troops and of the 1st Netherlands Army Corps, he was wounded at Waterloo. He later became King of Holland.*

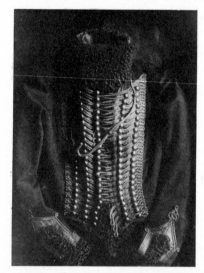

Black pelisse with gold braid decoration worn by the Prince of Orange on the 16th, 17th and 18th June 1815. Rijksmuseum, Amsterdam.

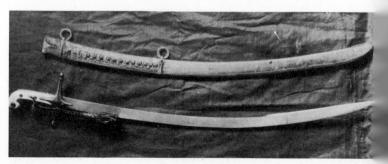

Oriental sabre, with scabbard covered in red velvet, carried by the Prince of Orange.

Prince William of Orange Nassau. By John Singleton Copley, R.A. Apsley House.

Major-General H.S.H. Prince Bernard of Saxe-Weimar, commander of the Dutch–Belgian 2nd Brigade (Perponcher's division). Drawing by Krabbe (1821), Musée Royal de l'Armée, Brussels. Major-

General Baron Charles Etienne de Ghigny, commander of the Dutch-Belgian 1st Light Cavalry Brigade. Lithograph by Roux, after an anonymous crayon sketch. Musée Royal de l'Armée, Brussels.

Major-General Baron J. V. de Constant Rebecque, 1794–1850, chief of staff of the Dutch-Belgian troops. Lithograph by E. Spanier, after I. H. Hoffmeister. Musée Royal de l'Armée, Brussels.

Lieutenant-General Baron D. H. Chassé, 1765–1849, commander of the Dutch-Belgian 3rd Division. Lithograph by E. Spanier, after I. H. Hoffmeister. Musée Royal de l'Armée, Brussels.

Lieutenant-General Baron H. G. de Perponcher-Sedlnitzky, commander of the Dutch-Belgian 2nd Division. Lithograph by E. Spanier, after I. H. Hoffmeister. Musée Royal de l'Armee, Brussels.

31

Light Infantry Corporal, Dutch-Belgian Troops. Lithograph by Canelle.

Chasseurs à Pied.
1, ex-velite of the Imperial Guard; 2, sergeant, flank company; 3, officer, chasseurs; 4, soldier, flank company; 5, bugler, battalion company; 6, bugler, flank company; 7, chevrons, corporal; 8, chevrons, sergeant; 9, shako; 10, officer's coatee; 11, French dragoon's musket (many of the light infantry units were equipped with the dragoon musket, pattern 1801/2); 12, wing, flank companies; 13, wing, buglers; 14, shako badge.

Carabinier Regiments.

1, 2nd Carabiniers (Belgian), sergeant; 2, 2nd Carabiniers (Belgian), trumpeter; 3, 2nd Carabiniers (Belgian), private; 4, 2nd Carabiniers (Belgian), officer wearing cloak; 5, 1st Carabiniers (Dutch), senior non-commissioned officer; 6, 3rd Carabiniers (Dutch), private; 7, 3rd Carabiniers (Dutch), trumpeter; 8, helmet of Belgian Carabinier; 9, saddle and valise of Carabinier; 10, private's sword; 10b, officer's sword; 11, coatee skirt, Belgian Carabinier; 12, hat, Dutch Carabinier; 13, trumpeter's "Swallow's Nest" or wing, Dutch Carabiniers.

fig N°10a

fig N°9

fig N°12

fig N°10b

fig N°13

fig N°11

fig N°5

fig N°7

fig N°1

fig N°2

fig N°3

fig N°4

fig N°6

fig N°8

Lloyd Beaufort 1965

4th and 5th Light Dragoons.

1, private in field dress, 4th Light Dragoons; 2, trumpeter in field dress, 4th Light Dragoons; 3, private (back view), 4th Light Dragoons; 4, officer, 5th Light Dragoons; 5, officer in field dress, 5th Light Dragoons; 6, trumpeter in field dress, 5th Light Dragoons; 7, private in field dress, 5th Light Dragoons; 8, officer, 4th Light Dragoons; 9, shako, 4th Regiment; 10a, shako, 5th Regiment; 10b, shako, officer, 5th Regiment; 11, equipment, officer of light dragoons; 12, shabraque, private, 5th Regiment; 13, chevrons, senior non-commissioned officer, and sword knot.

the United Netherlands

Horse Artillery.
1, sergeant; 2, gunner; 3, officer; 4, trumpeter (Dutch batteries); 5, corporal-trumpeter; 6, mounted gunner; 7, gunner's pouch and sword; 8, officer's pouch and sword; 9a, officer's epaulette; 9b, trumpeter's epaulette; 10, officer's belt; 11, gunner's shako. The Dutch-Belgian artillery consisted of nine batteries – seven Dutch and two Belgian – using 12- and 6-pounders. The Belgians had one horse battery, the Dutch two. All these batteries were equipped with 6-pounders except the reserve battery, which had a 12-pounder gun.

Infantry (Light and Line) of Duchy of Nassau.
1, fusilier, 2nd Nassau Light Infantry; 2, carabinier (grenadier), 2nd Nassau Light Infantry; 3, officer, 2nd Nassau Light Infantry; 4, officer of carabiniers (grenadiers), 2nd Nassau Light Infantry; 5, drummer, 2nd Nassau Light Infantry; 6, mounted officer; 7, coatee with waistcoat; 8, shako badge; 9, pouches, light infantry and carabiniers (grenadiers). A Nassau colour can be seen on page 30. Each battalion had its own colours carried by a grenadier sergeant, the point being gilded and bearing the cipher 'W'; the tassel and cords were also gilded, and the staff was made of darkened wood.

The Duchy of Nassau

The Duchy of Brunswick

At the outset of the 1815 campaign, the Duchy's army had just been reorganised. The old 'Black Legion' was still on foreign service. The new army consisted of 8 battalions: the 'Leib Battalion', the advance-guard battalion, 3 light infantry battalions and 3 line battalions; 5 cavalry squadrons, 4 hussar squadrons and 1 squadron of lancers, and 2 artillery batteries – one foot, one horse.

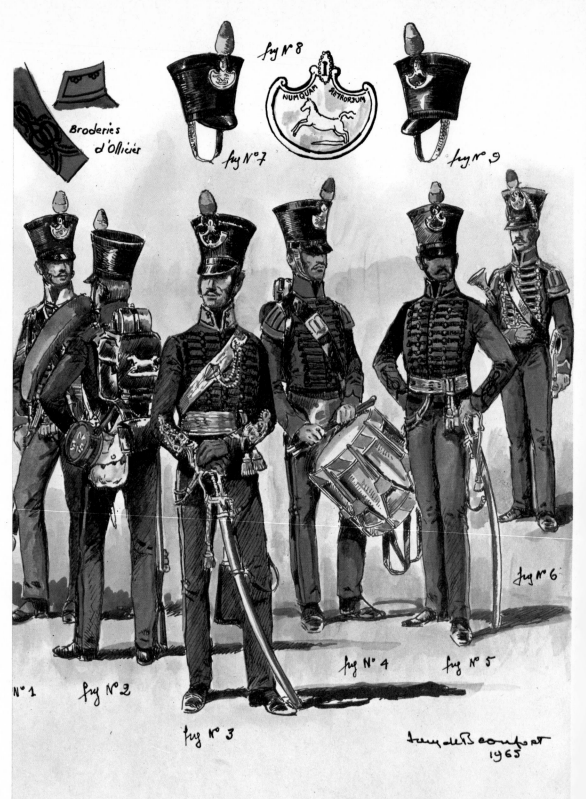

Colours of the 2nd and 3rd Battalions of the Line.

Each battalion had two colours of different sizes. The staffs, 3 metres long, had a point of leaf form with either the white horse of Brunswick and the ducal cipher or a coat of arms crowned with the letters 'F.W.' and the date – 1813 or 1814. Depending on the battalion, the tassel and cords were of silver and yellow or gold and blue. Only the battalions of the line had the colours.

Infantry of the Line and Light Infantry.

1, sergeant, 3rd Battalion of the line; 2, private, 2nd Battalion of the line; 3, field officer, 2nd light battalion; 4, drummer, 1st battalion of the line; 5, officer, 3rd light battalion; 6, bandsman, 1st battalion of the line; 7, private's shako, line battalions; 8, plate of line infantry shako; 9, light infantry shako.

The Prussian Army of the Lower Rhine

The standard of the 2nd Dragoons; below, guidon of the 1st Dragoons (formerly Regiment of Dragoons No. 7 Baczko).

Field-Marshal Prince Blücher von Wahlstadt, 1742–1819, *commander of the Army of the Lower Rhine. Painting by George Dawe, Apsley House.*
Often defeated by Napoleon but never discouraged, Prince von Wahlstadt was a valiant soldier. Nicknamed "Vorwärts" by his troops, in 1813 he personified the revival of the Prussian Army. In 1815 he was in command of the Army of the Lower Rhine. At Ligny, his horse was killed beneath him. It was due to his vigour that his troops arrived on the battlefield of Waterloo at the crucial moment, thereby turning an indecisive battle into a decisive victory.

Colonel von Clausewitz, 1780–1831, chief of staff of the 3rd Corps of the Army of the Lower Rhine. Lithograph by Michelis.

Lieutenant-General von Ziethen, commander of the 1st Corps of the Army of the Lower Rhine. Artist unknown. Musée Royal de l'Armée, Brussels.

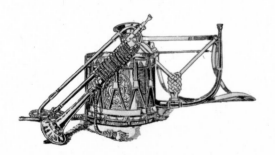

Left: Lieutenant-General Count Bülow von Dennewitz, 1755–1816, commander of the 4th Corps of the Army of the Lower Rhine. Engraving by Hullman. Musée Royal de l'Armée, Brussels.

The Army of the Lower Rhine was made up of remnants of the 1814 Prussian forces, concentrated in the region of Juliers, Luxembourg and the Wesel, reinforced by units of the standing army as well as the Landwehr (the territorial reserve), Westphalians, Saxons and others who had answered the king's call to arms of 7th April 1815. This army soon settled in around Liège and Namur, from where it could survey the frontier from Givet to Charleroi.

There were four corps: von Ziethen; von Pirch I; von Thielmann; and von Bülow. No reserves. 123,000 men and 304 pieces of artillery.

The army was rather inexperienced but aflame with patriotism. The infantry was, on the whole, well-trained but lacking in stamina and apt to tire quickly – and it was sometimes wasted by young, ardent officers who did not know how to use their troops to the best advantage. The cavalry was disciplined and well-mounted but not effectively used, being too dispersed. No one knows exactly what it did in the campaign. The artillery was weak and its draught was bad. Prussia was a poor country, and this was reflected in the simple – even dilapidated – uniforms of the troops. There is no record of how the Landwehr were equipped.

If the corps commanders were only second-rate – apart from Bülow, who was a good leader, though haughty and supercilious – Field-Marshal von Blücher, Commander-in-Chief of the Lower Rhine Army, instilled everyone with his own desperate sense of urgency, spurred on by his hatred for Napoleon and France and his desire for vengeance. Energetic, tenacious, crude, he put his doctrine into four words: "Vorwärts! Immer fester druff!" But his Chief of Staff, Count von Gneisenau – whom he used to call "the brains" – had military talents that matched his insufferable arrogance and conceit. For the latter qualities he was cordially detested by everyone – as was his deputy, General von Grolmann.

Behind these covering corps, there was a gradual build-up of troops: a Russian army (General Barclay de Tolly), 225,000 men in the Central Rhineland; an Austro-Bavarian army (Prince von Schwarzenberg), 250,000 men in the Upper Rhineland; an Italian army (General Frémont), 95,000 men in Piedmont. In the second line were the reserves . . . 800,000 men . . . a million men . . . no one knew.

Confronting such forces, France stood alone.

Lieutenant-General von Thielmann, commander of the 3rd Corps of the Army of the Lower Rhine.

Lieutenant-General Count von Gneisenau, 1760–1831, chief of staff of the Army of the Lower Rhine.

Prussian Infantry.

1, field officer; 2, senior non-commissioned officer carrying a colour; 3, musketeer; 4, subaltern, fusiliers; 5, drummer; 6, musketeer (rear view); 7, subaltern's epaulette; 8, infantry musket; 9, field officer's sword; 10, knapsack and kit; 11, cartridge pouch; 12, officer's waist sash; 13, subaltern's sword; 14, musketeer's short sword.

Colour of the 9th of the Line (2nd Pomeranians), 1808 model (with battle honour – Colberg, 1807).

The army of the Lower Rhine~Organisation

Commander-in-Chief: Field-Marshal Prince Blücher von Wahlstad.

Chief of Staff: Lieutenant-General Count von Gneisenau.

	Men
1st Corps: Lieutenant-General von Ziethen	
1st Brigade: Major-General von Steinmetz	9,000
2nd Brigade: Major-General von Pirch II	8,000
3rd Brigade: Major-General von Jagow	7,000
4th Brigade: Major-General Count Henckel von Donnersmarck	5,000
Cavalry Reserve: Major-General von Röder	2,000

Total: 29,000 foot, 2,000 horse and 88 artillery pieces.

2nd Corps: Major-General von Pirch I.	
5th Brigade: Major-General Count von Tippelskirch	7,000
6th Brigade: Major-General von Krafft	6,500
7th Brigade: Major-General von Brause	6,500
8th Brigade: Major-General von Bose	6,500
Cavalry Reserve: Major-General von Wahlen-Jürgass	4,400

Total: 26,000 foot, 4,000 horse and 80 artillery pieces.

3rd Corps: Lieutenant-General von Thielmann.	
Chief of Staff: Colonel von Clausewitz.	
9th Brigade: Major-General von Borcke	7,900
10th Brigade: Major-General von Kemphen	4,400
11th Brigade: Colonel von Luck	4,000
12th Brigade: Colonel von Stülpnagel	6,500
Cavalry Reserve: Major-General von Hobe	2,400

Total: 21,900 foot, 2,400 horse and 48 artillery pieces.

4th Corps: Infantry General Count Bülow von Dennewitz.	
13th Brigade: Lieutenant-General von Hacke	6,500
14th Brigade: Major-General von Ryssel	7,200
15th Brigade: Major-General von Losthin	7,000
16th Brigade: Colonel von Hiller	6,500
Cavalry Reserve: H.R.H. Prince William of Prussia	3,300

Total: 27,000 foot, 3,300 horse and 88 artillery pieces.

OVERALL TOTAL: 105,000 FOOT, 12,000 HORSE AND 219 GUNS.

Right: Colour of the 11th of the Line (1st Silesian). Former 33rd Regiment.

Schützen and Jäger Volunteers.

1, bugler, Silesian Jägers; 2, the same, wearing full dress uniform; 2b, officer, Silesian Jägers; 3, Silesian Jäger; 4, Volunteer, Silesian Jägers (attached to the 10th and 11th Regiments of the Line – 1st and 2nd Silesians); 5, Volunteer Jäger, 1st Pomeranians (20th Infantry Regiment); 6, Volunteer Jäger, West Prussians (attached to the 2nd West Prussians, 7th Infantry Regiment); 7, turn-back detail; 8, arms and equipment of Jägers and Schützen; 9a, private's full dress shako; 9b, officer's shako; 9c, shoulder braid and aiguillettes.

Landwehr Cavalry Regiments.

1, sergeant, Silesian Landwehr Detachment, Freiwillige Jäger; 2, trooper, Silesian Landwehr Cavalry; 3, trooper, Elbe Landwehr Cavalry; 4, trooper, Silesian Landwehr; 5, Uhlan, Silesian Landwehr Cavalry (1815 Regulations); 6, officer, Elbe Landwehr; 7, 8, Silesian Landwehr cavalry, 7th and 3rd Regiment sergeants; 9, Kollet of Silesian Landwehr and Uhlans; 10, 'Czapka' of Silesian Landwehr and Uhlans.

The Prussians

Dragoon Regiments.

1, officer, Queen's Regiment; 2, officer, Brandenburg Regiment; 3, dragoon, Queen's Regiment, wearing a 'Litewka'; 4, senior non-commissioned officer, Brandenburg Regiment; 5, dragoon, Neumarck Regiment; 6, trumpeter, Neumarck Regiment; 7, other ranks' shako; 8, shabraque; 9, other ranks' pouch; 10, officer's forage cap; 11, dragoon's sword.

Colour of the 6th Infantry Regiment (1st West Prussians – the former von Rheenhardt No. 52).

Silesian Landwehr.
1, private, 1815; 2, drummer; 3, private; 4, private (rear view); 5, officer; 6, sergeant; 7, other ranks' forage cap; 8, sergeant's collar; 9, iron cross; 10, officer's forage cap; 11, shoulder strap.

Hussars.
1, hussar of the 4th Regiment (1st Silesian Hussars); 2, Freiwillige Jäger attached to the 6th Regiment of Hussars (2nd Silesian Hussars). This squadron wore the pelisses taken from the 2nd French Hussars at Nancy in 1814. 3, Freiwillige Jäger attached to the 10th Regiment of Hussars; 4, hussar, 5th Regiment of Hussars (the Pomeranian Hussars); 5, trumpeter, 6th Regiment of Hussars (2nd Silesian Hussars); 6, officer, 6th Regiment of Hussars (2nd Silesian Hussars); 7, trumpeter, 3rd Regiment of Hussars (the Brandenburg Hussars); 8, hussar's shako; 9, sabretache, 6th Regiment of Hussars (2nd Silesian Hussars); 10a, officer's sword; 10b sword (other ranks); 10c, carbine; 11, horse furniture.

The French Army of the North

Unable for political reasons to reintroduce conscription, Napoleon had to be satisfied with 150,000 men including 28,000 cavalry left by the King. This number was swelled by 12,000 officers and 85,000 soldiers made up from those who had been on leave, in retirement, in the reserve, etc., and the recalling of the Imperial Guard, the raising of the National Guard and the ringing of the tocsin to summon the French nation to arms. In ten weeks, Napoleon assembled some 290,000 men on active service and 220,000 auxiliaries. He flung seven small observation corps to the frontier to delay the enemy should this prove necessary, left garrisons at places where there had not been enough time to get them in

Napoleon I. Sketch by Robert Lefèvre.

fighting trim, and formed a campaign army under his personal command:

Five corps: 1st, General Count Drouet d'Erlon; 2nd General Count Reille; 3rd, General Count Vandamme; 4th, General Count Gérard; 6th, General Mouton, Count of Lobau. The Imperial Guard. Cavalry reserves, Marshal Count Grouchy. A total of 125,000 men including 18,500 mounted troops, with 374 pieces of artillery.

The infantry was good, with a fine offensive spirit, and it manoeuvred well. The cavalry was excellent, well-trained and under the command of capable officers. The gunners, so it was claimed, were the best in the world when it came to speed and accuracy of fire.

The Imperial Guard consisted of eight infantry regiments of the Old Guard: four of chasseurs and four of grenadiers; eight of the Young Guard: four of voltigeurs and four of tirailleurs; four cavalry regiments of the Old Guard: chasseurs, lancers, dragoons, grenadiers; two regiments of artillery of the Old Guard – one foot and one horse; an infantry battalion of the Young Guard; and engineers, gendarmes, service auxiliaries, etc., making, in all, 20,000 crack troops.

It was a tough army, numbering in its ranks men who had grown old in quest of victory: those who had been taken prisoner in Russia, Spain and Germany and who had been repatriated the previous year with wrongs to avenge. War-hardened, disciplined – these were men who had already proved their courage and their worth. The 'Marie-Louise' troops of 1814 were old soldiers. Their morale was high; the refrains that yesterday had been hummed under their breath were now shouted at the top of their voices . . . "The Emperor is invincible! He will not let himself be taken by the plotting of traitors!" As contemporary publications show, treason was currently on everyone's mind. "There is madness in the air," an English spy wrote from Paris.

The army was well supplied with excellent regimental officers. The old ones who had been on half-pay eagerly returned to resume their former careers, imbued with a sense of duty and the cult of honour. Generals were hastily appointed from among those who still had a career to make: Drouet d'Erlon, who had done well in Spain; Reille, who was

Marshal Soult, Duke of Dalmatia, 1769–1851. By Alexander Healy. Apsley House.
Created marshal in 1804, he played an important part in the Peninsular War. He went over to Louis XVIII and became Minister of War during the first Restoration. Despite the defamatory proclamation issued on the Emperor's return from Elba, Napoleon conferred on him the key post of Chief of Staff in the Army of the North. This selection for an office he had never before filled was to have disastrous consequences.

Marshal Ney, Duke of Elchingen, Prince of the Moscova, 1769–1815, commander of the 1st and 2nd Corps of the Army of the North. Created marshal in 1804, he took part in all the campaigns of the revolution and the Empire. Nicknamed "the bravest of the brave", he covered himself with glory commanding the rear-guard during the retreat from Russia. In 1814, he was one of the marshals who forced the Emperor to abdicate. On the Emperor's return from Elba he accepted a command from Louis XVIII to block Napoleon's advance, but instead he went over to Napoleon. He rejoined the army only on 15th June, and Napoleon entrusted him with the command of the 1st and 2nd Corps.

a veteran of the Italian campaign and had commanded a division at Wagram; Vandamme – brusque, quarrelsome, conscientious; Gérard – the only one who had previously commanded an army corps; Mouton – excellent at deploying infantry; Pajol – the most outstanding of the light horse; Exelmans – intrepid, brilliant, high-minded and quick-tempered; Kellermann – a first-class cavalry tactician; Milhaud, whose ability and courage only became apparent on the battlefield . . .

"Don't use the marshals," an old soldier wrote to the Emperor. There were so few of them left. Most of them were dead, in exile, 'struck off the list', discarded, too old; but for reasons of prestige the Emperor wanted to have those who were still available near him: Mortier, cavalry commandant of the Guard who was to fall ill before the campaign started; Grouchy, newly appointed; Devout, Minister of War; Ney, who would only be called upon as a last resort; even Soult, who had betrayed the Emperor in 1814 – an ardent apologist before royalty in order to be appointed the King's Minister of War, then abject disparager of the Bourbons after Napoleon's return from Elba and subsequently the accuser of Drouet d'Erlon, Exelmans, Lefebvre-Desnoëttes – compared by Vandamme to Marmont. Although he was in bad repute with the army despite his past victories, Soult was appointed Chief of Staff . . . Napoleon knew that certain generals would not shake hands with Soult or even salute him, but he believed that he could impose his selection on them on the strength of his own prestige. For this key post that the Duke of Dalmatia was incapable of filling, why did the Emperor not designate General Bailly de Monthion, long-time aide to Berthier, who had the experience for this exceptionally critical task?

The uniform of the marching columns might have been shabby, but the copper badge, with its Imperial Eagle, gleamed on their headgear. Dug out from the depths of cupboards, the 'cuckoo' – which had been seen once before on the previous 15th August – returned to the shakos, the bearskins

45

Lieutenant-General.

Officer of Carabiniers.

Officer of the 5th Hussars.

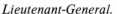

Marshal Mortier, Duke of Treviso, *1768–1835. Painting by Larivière.*

and the helmets. Breaches of regulations were condoned to allow offenders to flatten the fleur-de-lys with hammers and cut the Bourbon emblems from their uniforms. Well-polished, the touched-up insignia served only to highlight the miserable condition of the overcoats, cloaks and undress caps that had been resurrected at the call of the 'Tondu' from the booths, barns and sheds where their owners had, by strenuous exertions, been eking out a living . . . Now the resurrected insignia embellished the wide trousers made from coarse canvas and the multi-coloured clothes that had been hastily cut out, tacked together and sewn in small workshops in the short space of ten weeks. The punctilious might brandish the 1812 Regulations, but everyone else had more important fish to fry . . . Civilian frock-coats with tarnished epaulettes and military buttons were to be seen here and there among the command of armies, reminding the old-timers – as well as d'Erlon, Reille, Vandamme, and even the Emperor himself – of the days of their youth in 1796.

Volunteered in 1791, Mortier was to serve in the Army of the North, the Army of the Sambre and Meuse, and the Army of the Rhine. He became a marshal in 1804 and distinguished himself on all the battlefields of the Empire. During the Hundred Days he was appointed Commander of the Imperial Guard Cavalry, but he did not take up his post as he fell ill on the eve of the campaign.

...cer of the Chasseurs à Pied of the Young Guard.   *Cuirassier of the 4th Regiment.*   *Voltigeur of the Infantry of the Line.*

Colour illustrations: Collection of the Musée de l'Armée, Château de l'Emperi.

The 1st Chasseurs à Cheval went into action wearing the helmets of a royal regiment. There was a shortage of blue cloth for greatcoats, but green or maroon was better than nothing at all. The cavalry was in better shape, but some cuirassier regiments – particularly the 11th – lacked cuirasses.

The Old Guard was better groomed, with blue half-belted greatcoats, bearskins and white leather straps and belts. The 'Middle Guard' – the 3rd and 4th Grenadiers and Chasseurs – wore the shako; but some of the gun and pouch straps had to be improvised from twisted string . . . (A Prussian general mistook the 4th Grenadiers for the National Guard and carelessly attacked them, which he was to repent . . . in the next world.) Officers wore an overcoat and blue trousers; and generals had jackets decorated with braid, and breeches of the same colour.

The Emperor kept to his legendary uniform: the grey riding coat made from such light material that it looked like a dust-coat. His 'household' was modest in the extreme: Count

After 1813, Count de la Bédoyère, a brilliant officer, was twice proposed for the rank of general during the French campaign. Commandant of the 7th Line Regiment, he went over to Napoleon during his march on Grenoble, and became General Aide-de-Camp to the Emperor at Waterloo. He was shot at the outset of the second Restoration after a summary trial.

Brigadier-General Count de la Bédoyère, *1786–1815, aide-de-camp to the Emperor. Miniature after Guérin. Collection of Madame Reimbert de la Bédoyère.*

Grenadiers of the Imperial Guard.
1, grenadier in greatcoat; 2, grenadier in greatcoat (rear view); 3, officer in marching order; 4, officer in undress coat; 5, eagle-bearer officer; 6, grenadier in marching order; 7, cartridge pouch; 8, musket of the Guard; 9, officer's sword; 10, bearskin plaque; 11, officer's scale; 12, short sword (sabre briquet) for other ranks; 13, sword-belt plaque.

Bertrand the Grand-Marshal; the aides-de-camp; the Chamberlain de Turenne; the equerries Fouler de Relingue, de Mesgrigny, de Briel; three pages; the Duke of Bassano; the First Secretary Baron de Fain; the surgeon Yvan; a few servants; and a train of only ten carriages.

The trained army was brave, but there was an inevitable lack of cohesion because the men did not know their commanders and distrusted the generals. Quick to take offence, nervy, in the grip of the emotions of 1794, vibrating with passionate devotion to the Emperor, it was capable of reaching the heights of ecstasy and, equally, plumbing the depths of depression.

The French

Chasseurs à Pied of the Imperial Guard.
1, sergeant in marching order; 2, chasseur in greatcoat, marching order; 3, chasseur in field dress; 4, officer in undress; 5, sapper in overcoat, marching order; 6, sapper in field dress; 7, chasseur's coat-tail detail; 8, sapper's carbine; 9, officer's epaulette; 10, officer's hat; 11, cockade taking form of a pompom; 12, officer's gorget, decoration; 13, sapper's belt plate; 14, detail on officer's overcoat-tail. On his return from Elba, the Emperor reorganised the Imperial Guard. The Infantry of the Guard, comprising the grenadiers and the chasseurs, formed the Old Guard and the Middle Guard; and the tirailleurs and voltigeurs formed the Young Guard.

The French

fig nº 11

fig nº 10

fig nº 8

fig nº 9

fig nº 12

fig nº 6

fig nº 7

fig nº 1

Terry de Beaufort
1970

fig nº 2

fig nº 3

fig nº 4

fig nº 5

Lancers (Chevau-Legers-Lanciers).

1, trooper of the élite company of the 1st Regiment; 2, sergeant-major of the 1st Regiment; 3, officer of the 1st Regiment in field dress; 4, colonel of the 6th Regiment; 5, trooper of the élite company of the 6th Regiment; 6, trooper of the 3rd Regiment; 7, trumpeter of the 1st Regiment; 8, trooper's saddle-cloth; 9, trooper's helmet; 10, coatee of officer of the 1st Regiment; 11, lancer's accoutrements; 12, officer's helmet.

Standard of the 10th Regiment of Cuirassiers.

Cuirassier Regiments.
1, cuirassier in riding cloak; 2, cuirassier of the 12th Regiment; 3, sergeant of the 7th Regiment in police cap; 4, cuirassier of the 11th Regiment; 5, trumpeter of the 9th Regiment; 6, trumpeter of the 1st Regiment; 7, lieutenant of the 1st Regiment; 8, officer's cuirass; 9, cuirassier of the 1st Regiment; 10a, officer's sword; 10b, trooper's sword; 11, officer's helmet. Cuirassier regiments present at Waterloo were the 1st, 2nd, 3rd, 4th, 5th, 6th, 7th, 8th, 9th, 10th, 11th, and 12th.

Standard of the 6th Regiment of Chasseurs à Cheval.

Chasseurs à Cheval.

1, chasseur of the élite company of the 4th Regiment, in cloak; 2, officer, 1st Chasseurs à Cheval; 3, corporal, élite company of the 1st Chasseurs; 4, chasseur, élite company of the 6th Regiment; 5, non-commissioned officer, 6th Chasseurs à Cheval; 6, chasseur, 6th Regiment in field dress; 7, officer's helmet, 1st Chasseurs à Cheval; 8, officer's shako, pouches, sword, chasseurs à cheval (royal livery); 9, trumpeter, 1st Chasseurs à Cheval; 10, other ranks' helmet, 1st Chasseurs à Cheval; 11, officer, élite company of the 6th Chasseurs. Due to insufficiency of supplies, the 1st Regiment of the Chasseurs à Pied went into the Waterloo campaign in the royal cavalry uniform. Although the chasseurs hammered the arms of France on their helmets, the trumpeters kept to the king's livery.

Lancers of the Guard.

1, officer of the 1st (Polish) Squadron; 2, lancer of the 1st (Polish) Squadron; 3, General de Colbert, regimental commander; 4, officer of the left flank squadrons; 5, corporal of the left flank squadrons; 6, lancer of the left flank squadrons; 7, trumpeter of the 1st (Polish) Squadron; 8, trumpeter of the left flank squadrons; 9, aiguillettes; 10, 'Czapka' of General de Colbert; 11, 'Czapka' of Captain Soufflot, worn at Waterloo.

52

The army of the north~ Organisation

THE EMPEROR: Commander-in-Chief.

Household: Lieutenant-General Count Bertrand, Grand Marshal of the Palace.

Aides-de-camp: Generals Lebrun, Drouot, Corbineau, de Flahaut, Dejean, Bernard, de La Bédoyère.

Personal Staff: Colonel Gourgaud and 12 officers.

Master of the Horse: General Fouler de Telingue and 3 equerries.

Chamberlain: Viscount Turenne.

Sergeant of Mounted Troops: de Guerchy.
    12 pages.

Imperial War Cabinet: Maret, Duke of Bassano.

Secretaries: Baron Fain, Fleury de Chaboulon.

Surgeon: Baron Yvan.

General Headquarters

Chief of Staff for the Army: Marshal Soult.

Chief of Headquarters Staff: Lieutenant-General Bailly de Monthion.

3 Deputy Chiefs of the General Staff. 4 senior staff officers. 30 assistant staff officers.

Artillery: Lieutenant-General Ruty.

Engineers: Lieutenant-General Rogniat.

Topographical department: Colonel Bonne.

Gendarmerie: Lieutenant-General Radet.

Medical Department: Chief-Surgeon Percy.

3 supernumerary generals.

Imperial Guard

Lieutenant-General Count Drouot, Deputy Chief of Staff for the Army.

Infantry of the Old Guard.

Grenadiers: Lieutenant-Generals Friant and Roguet.
    1st Grenadiers: Brigadier-General Petit.
    2nd Grenadiers: Brigadier-General Christiani.
    3rd Grenadiers: Brigadier-General Poret de Morvan.
    4th Grenadiers: Brigadier-General Harlet (1 battalion).
Total of 7 battalions: 3,800 men

Chasseurs: Lieutenant-Generals Morand and Michel.
    1st Chasseurs: Brigadier-General Cambronne.
    2nd Chasseurs: Brigadier-General Pelet.
    3rd Chasseurs: Brigadier-General Mallet.
    4th Chasseurs: Brigadier-General Henrion.
Total of 8 battalions: 4,600 men

(The 3rd and 4th Grenadiers and Chasseurs were sometimes known as the Middle Guard.)

Infantry of the Young Guard: Lieutenant-General Duhesme, commanding the 1st and 2nd Divisions.
1st Division: Lieutenant-General Barrois.
    1st Brigade: Brigadier-General Chartrand. (1st Tirailleurs, 1st Voltigeurs).
    2nd Brigade: Brigadier-General Guye. (3rd Tirailleurs, 3rd Voltigeurs).
Total of 8 battalions: 4,200 men

Cavalry: Commander-in-Chief, Marshal Mortier, Duke of Treviso (did not rejoin).
Old Guard.
    Light Cavalry: Lieutenant-General Lefebvre-Desnoëttes.
    Cavalry Reserve: Lieutenant-General Guyot. 4,000 horse

Artillery: Commander-in-Chief: Lieutenant-General Desvaux de Saint-Maurice.
Old Guard.
    Foot: Brigadier-General Lallemand.
    Horse: Colonel Duchand.   2,000

Young Guard.
    6 batteries, not in regiments   1,000
    Reserve batteries. In all, 118 guns.
Waggon train   300
Engineers: Lieutenant-General Haxo   125
Marines: Frigate-Captain Tailhade   147
Gendarmerie d'élite. 1st Company (Old Guard): Captain Duyonnet   106

1st Corps

Commander-in-Chief: Lieutenant-General Drouet d'Erlon.
Chief of Staff: Brigadier-General Delcambre.
1st Division: Lieutenant-General Allix (absent). Replaced by: Brigadier-General Quiot.
    Brigade Quiot. 54th and 55th of the Line
    Brigade Bourgeois. 28th and 105th of the Line   4,000
2nd Division: Lieutenant-General Donzelot.
    Brigade Schmitz. 13th Light and 17th Line
    Brigade Aulard, 19th and 51st Line   4,500
3rd Division: Lieutenant-General Marcognet.
    Brigade Noguès. 21st and 46th Line
    Brigade Grenier. 25th and 45th Line   4,000

4th Division: Lieutenant-General Durutte.
    Brigade Pégot. 8th and 29th Line
    Brigade Brue. 85th and 95th Line   4,000
1st Cavalry Division: Lieutenant-General Jacquinot.
    Brigade Bruno. 7th Hussars and 3rd Chasseurs à Cheval
    Brigade Gobrecht. 3rd and 4th Lancers   1,800
Reserve Artillery   200
Engineers, sappers   350
    6 batteries   ———
        20,950

2nd Corps

Commander-in-Chief: Lieutenant-General Reille.
Chief of Staff: Lieutenant-General Pamphile Lacroix.
5th Division: Lieutenant-General Bachelu.
    Brigade Husson. 2nd Light and 61st Line
    Brigade Campi. 72nd and 108th Line   5,000
6th Division: Lieutenant-General Prince Jérôme Napoléon.
    Brigade Bauduin. 1st Light and 3rd Line
    Brigade Soye. 1st and 2nd Line   6,500
7th Division: Lieutenant-General Girard.
    Brigade de Villiers. 11th Light and 82nd Line
    Brigade Piat. 12th Light and 4th Line   5,000
9th Division: Lieutenant-General Foy.
    Brigade Gauthier. 92nd and 93rd Line
    Brigade Jamin. 4th Light and 100th Line   5,300
2nd Cavalry Division: Lieutenant-General Piré.
    Brigade Hubert. 1st and 2nd Chasseurs à Cheval
    Brigade Wathiez. 5th and 6th Lancers   1,800
Artillery, 6 batteries   ———
        23,000

3rd Corps

Commander-in-Chief: Lieutenant-General Vandamme.
Chief of Staff: Brigadier-General Revest.
8th Division: Lieutenant-General Lefol.
    Brigade Billiard. 15th Light and 23rd Line
    Brigade Corsin. 37th and 64th Line   5,000
10th Division: Lieutenant-General Habert.
    Brigade Gengoult. 34th and 88th Line
    Brigade Dupeyroux. 22nd and 70th Line, and 2nd Swiss   5,500
11th Division: Lieutenant-General Berthezène.
    Brigade Dufour. 12th and 56th Line

Brigade Lagarde. 33rd and 86th Line   4,500
3rd Cavalry Division: Lieutenant-General Domon.
   Brigade Dommanget. 4th and 9th Chasseurs à Cheval
   Brigade Vinot. 12th Chasseurs à Cheval   1,000
Artillery, 5 batteries   ——
    17,150

4th Corps

Commander-in-Chief: Lieutenant-General Gérard.
Chief of Staff: Brigadier-General Saint-Rémy.
12th Division: Lieutenant-General Pécheux.
   Brigade Rome. 30th and 96th Line
   Brigade Schoeffer. 6th Light and 63rd Line   4,700
13th Division: Lieutenant-General Vichery.
   Brigade Le Capitaine. 59th and 76th Line
   Brigade Desprez. 48th and 69th Line   4,000
14th Division: Lieutenant-General Bourmont
   (deserted to the enemy).
   Brigade Hulot. 9th Light and 111th Line   4,200
   Brigade Toussaint. 44th and 50th Line   4,200
7th Cavalry Division: Lieutenant-General Maurin,
   then Vallin.
   Brigade Vallin. 6th Hussars and 8th Chasseurs à
   Cheval
   Brigade Berruyer. 6th and 16th Dragoons   1,600
Artillery, 5 batteries   ——
    15,700

6th Corps

Commander-in-Chief: Lieutenant-General Mouton.
Chief of Staff: Brigadier-General Durrier.
19th Division: Lieutenant-General Simmer.
   Brigade Bellair. 5th and 11th Line
   Brigade Jamin. 27th and 84th Line   4,000
20th Division: Lieutenant-General Jeanin.
   Brigade Bony. 5th Light and 10th Line
   Brigade de Tromelin. 47th and 107th Line   3,000
21st Division: Lieutenant-General Teste.
   Brigade Lafitte. 8th Light and 40th Line
   Brigade Penne. 65th and 75th Line   2,400
Artillery, 4 batteries   ——
    10,300

Cavalry Reserve

1ST CORPS: Lieutenant-General Pajol.
4th Division: Lieutenant-General Soult.

Brigade Houssin de St. Laurent. 1st and 4th
   Hussars
Brigade Ameil. 5th Hussars   1,300
5th Division: Lieutenant-General Subervie.
   Brigade A. de Colbert. 1st and 2nd Lancers
   Brigade Merlin de Douai. 11th Chasseurs à Cheval   1,200
Artillery, 2 batteries   ——
    2,800

2ND CORPS Lieutenant-General Exelmans.
9th Division: Lieutenant-General Strolz.
   Brigade Burthe. 5th and 13th Dragoons
   Brigade Vincent. 15th and 20th Dragoons   1,600
10th Division: Lieutenant-General Chastel.
   Brigade Bonnemains. 4th and 12th Dragoons
   Brigade Berton. 14th and 17th Dragoons
Artillery, 2 batteries   1.400
    3,290

3RD CORPS: Lieutenant-General Kellermann.
11th Division: Lieutenant-General L'Héritier.
   Brigade Picquet. 2nd and 7th Dragoons
   Brigade Guiton. 8th and 11th Cuirassiers   1,800
12th Division: Lieutenant-General Roussel d'Hurbal.
   Brigade Blancard, 1st and 2nd Carabiniers
   Brigade Donop. 2nd and 3rd Cuirassiers   1,600
Artillery, 2 batteries   ——
    3,700

4TH CORPS: Lieutenant-General Milhaud.
13th Division: Lieutenant-General Wathier de
   St-Alphonse.
   Brigade Dubois. 1st and 4th Cuirassiers
   Brigade Travers. 7th and 12th Cuirassiers   1,100
14th Division: Lieutenant-General Delort.
   Brigade Farine. 5th and 10th Cuirassiers
   Brigade Vial. 6th and 9th Cuirassiers   1,600
Artillery, 2 batteries   ——
    3,000

TOTAL: 112,468 MEN (90,000 FOOT, 22,000 HORSE AND 366 GUNS).

The Allied plan of campaign

Wellington.

Field-Marshal Blücher and General Bülow.

The 'Armée du Nord' had been on the march towards the frontier since 6th June. The Emperor, who had been hesitating between defence and offence, seemed at last to have reached a decision.

The armies of the Low Countries and the Lower Rhine were stretched along a wide frontier from the sea to Givet.

The Anglo-Netherlands army occupied a front that was 80 kilometres wide and 50 kilometres deep. Headquarters: Wellington in Brussels; the Prince of Orange at Braine-le-Comte; Lord Hill at Grammont.

The Lower Rhine Army held a front that was 60 kilometres wide and 50 kilometres deep. Headquarters: Blücher in Namur; Ziethen in Charleroi; Pirch I in Namur; Thielmann in Ciney; Bulow at Liège.

Liaison between the commanders of the two armies was effected by special emissaries: the English Colonel Sir H. Hardinge with Blücher, the Prussian General von Müffling with Wellington.

On the assumption that there would be a general Allied offensive against Paris between 1st and 15th July, in accordance with Prince von Schwarzenberg's plan, the two army commanders had not drawn up any joint defensive plan and had made no arrangements to provide each other with mutual assistance in the event of attack. Moreover, their contact with each other was purely formal.

"Do not trust Wellington," Gneisenau said to von Müffling when he was leaving. "He is a master of deceit."

"I hope you will not often have need of me," the Duke wrote to the Prussian General.

Wellington quietly assumed control of military matters without appearing to do so, and certainly without ever boasting about it.

The Emperor was informed of the enemy's plans through his own and Fouché's spies, from the Swiss press and the *Frankfurter Gazette*. His decision was an offensive in Belgium aimed at the destruction of the armies of Wellington and Blücher before the Russians, Austrians and others could get to the front.

Consequently, the corps of the Armée du Nord were assembled between Rocroi and Avesnes. It was all top secret – "not even a hare may cross the frontier".

Napoleon's plan of campaign

The Emperor.

Sunday, 11th June. Last mass at the Tuileries. A few audiences: Davout summoned Marshal Ney to Avesnes "if he wanted to be at the first battles"; a walk in the garden, a family dinner . . . "Let us hope, Madame Bertrand, that we shall have no cause to regret the Isle of Elba," Napoleon said, on taking his leave.

On the 12th, at 4 a.m., he left the Elysée with the Duke of Bassano and General Bertrand, lunched at Soissons and slept at Laon. Grouchy was there. Why had the cavalry not set off? Soult had omitted to send marching orders.

Napoleon still had time to decide on his 'method' – offensive or defensive – in selecting his terrain for a national war. He would personally have preferred a national war, but the French Chamber of Representatives, the liberals, the ideologists, the 'Constitutionalists' and La Fayette had begun to have misgivings: ruled by politics the sovereign had to impose silence on the war-leader. Occupied with enemies inside and outside France, he had first to vanquish the latter in order to win over the former. "He would have done better not to have recalled Parliament," General Foy was to write, adding: "He has gone to join the army in a melancholy mood and filled with dark forebodings."

Stake everything to win . . .

This was the true malady from which he suffered. Despite a kidney disease, his activity and stamina were prodigious during the eighty-five days of his last reign and the ninety-six hours of the campaign. Yet it seemed at times as if there was a shadow between him and the real world. His imagination and conceit overcame him and upset the balance of his judgement. There was no deterioration in his lucidity or in the keenness of his intellect, but after April 1814 his energy sometimes appeared to flag: he took longer to make a decision; he meditated, hesitating as if he were rather tired or unsure of himself; and this state was expressed by silences and lack of resolution that no one had the temerity to challenge.

"Me quoque fata regunt" – "I also am a pawn of destiny", as Ovid had Jupiter declare . . .

Napoleon no longer had the same faith in his star, and he tried to conceal his uncertainties behind authoritative statements, a contempt for his adversaries, a kind of arrogant confusion between the wish and the deed . . .

Types of Prussian soldiers. By Knötel.

Quarters of the Life Guards. Drawing by James Thirair, from a commemorative album of the battle of Waterloo.

"The Asides of Glory." Charlet. Private collection.

The armies march...

French infantry on the march. Drawing by Detaille. Musée de l'Armée, Paris.

When he arrived at the vicarage of Avesnes on the 13th, Napoleon knew exactly what forces were at his disposal. All the available information was placed before him, maps were spread out, and he meditated . . .

The British and Prussian armies were immobile along 150 kilometres of frontier on both sides of Charleroi – the former looking towards Ostend and the latter towards the Rhine.

The communications route between them was on the line Nivelles, Quatre-Bras, Namur. But the Charleroi-Brussels road intersected this at Quatre-Bras, thus separating the two armies . . .

The psychological factor was that Wellington and Blücher were only mediocre strategists. Wellington was skilful in defence but not much good at manoeuvres – slow to get going, prudent, practical, egotistical; Blücher, the fiery Hussar with "Vorwärts" on his lips, was a firm believer in attacking with the utmost force, setting off at a gallop as soon as he heard gunfire. The two men had one thing in common:

The French offensive of 14th, 15th and 16th June

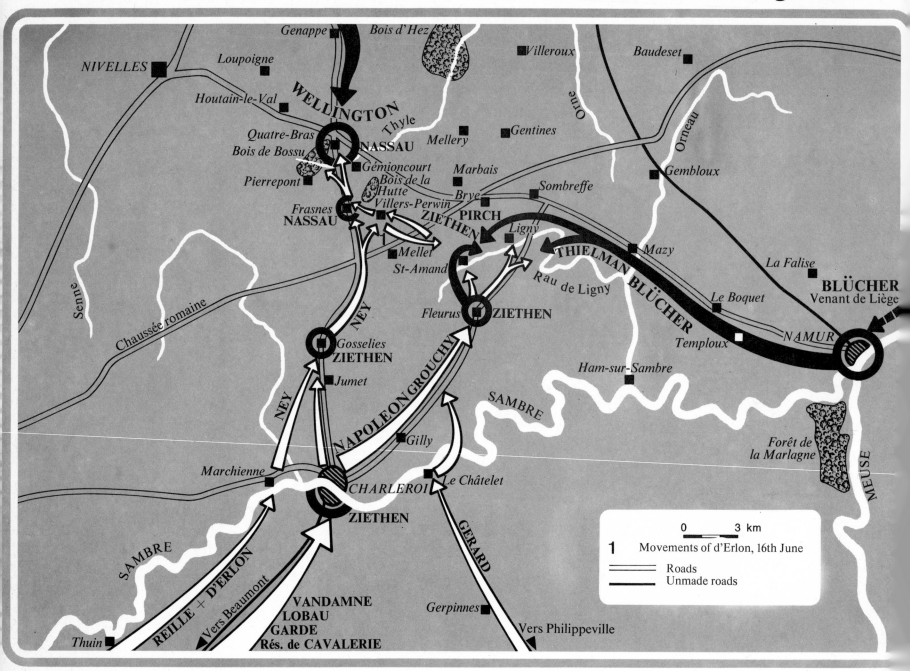

The Charleroi region was the key point linking Blücher's advance posts with those of Wellington. Their headquarters, at Namur and Brussels respectively, were sixty-four kilometres apart. It was here, therefore, that Napoleon decided to invade with the aim of cutting the Brussels–Namur road in the Sombreffe–Quatre-Bras sector to accomplish the separation of the two Allied armies.

After crossing the Sambre river on the 15th, the French were unsuccessful on the 16th in completely executing their plan. In fact, Ney's left flank was thrown back from Quatre-Bras to Frasnes; and Napoleon, on the right flank, encountered stiff resistance from three Prussian corps behind the Ligny stream. Nevertheless, Napoleon's partial victory at Ligny did prevent an immediate link-up between Wellington and Blücher.

persistence – cold in the Briton and brutal in the Prussian.

Napoleon kept his thoughts to himself. On the morning of the 14th June, however, he wrote to his brother Joseph: "This evening I shall be moving the Imperial Headquarters to Beaumont. Tomorrow, the 15th, I shall go to Charleroi, where the Prussian army is positioned, which will mean a battle or a retreat by the enemy." And to Davout, Minister of War, he wrote: "I shall cross the Sambre tomorrow, the 15th. If the Prussians do not fall back, we shall have a battle."

The Emperor decided to muster the French Army around Beaumont in a solid mass, storm Charleroi, cross the Sambre at this point, and take the Prussians by surprise and defeat them.

Thus on the evening of the 14th he was installed in the château of the Prince of Caraman-Chimay at Beaumont – a large village on a hillock, surrounded by a small river and situated in the centre of a wooded region left in French hands under the treaties of 1814.

It was raining: the bivouacs were flooded. The infantry of the Guard, in three lines, were floundering in the mud about a quarter of a league in front of Beaumont: the cavalry were in the rear.

The 2nd Corps (Reille) was at Leers-Forteau, near the frontier: its cavalry, which was ahead, was ready to move. The 1st Corps (d'Erlon) was at Solre-sur-Sambre. Fires were carefully concealed from view, the bivouacs being set up behind stacked arms and drums; from their donkeys or barrows, the sutlers handed out 'nips' to the men.

The 3rd Corps was a league in front of Beaumont, near the frontier. Withdrawal was forbidden.

The 6th Corps was a quarter of a league away from the 3rd. Horses were watered; gunners presented their equipment to their officers for inspection: sponges, buckets, portfires; ammunition waggons were opened up.

Marshal Grouchy's four corps under Pajol, Exelmans, Kellermann and Milhaud were deployed between Beaumont and Walcourt, ready to reconnoitre the army's road to Charleroi.

The 4th Corps (Gérard) and Delort's cuirassier division of the 4th Cavalry Corps, at Philippeville, were ready to move off at dawn to join up with the 3rd Corps in support of the advance on Charleroi. The last troops came down from the mist-drenched woods.

In the evening there was singing . . .

At roll-call the army numbered 122,408 men equipped with 374 guns, in a rectangle measuring 8 leagues by 2 leagues, on the outskirts of a forest behind which Ziethen's outposts were on the alert.

They had been warned.

Wellington no longer believed in anything or anybody but himself: Napoleon would certainly conduct a defensive action elsewhere . . . And seeming unconcerned, he was reassured by messages from his advance posts: "All is calm." That was the main thing. Preparations could go ahead for celebrating the victory of 21st June 1813 at Vittoria, and also for the ball to be given on the 15th in Brussels by the Duke and Duchess of Richmond. 'Boney' and his bearskins were far away . . .

Since the 9th, the British had known that the French corps were gathering between Avesnes and Philippeville; but they were reluctant to believe the reports. "We are too strong to be attacked here," Wellington proclaimed. "Bonaparte will not attack us," predicted Blücher.

Fouché actually sent the Duke the battle order of the Armée du Nord; but fearing for his life, he had the messenger stopped before he could reach the frontier.

Then scraps of information – numerous and contradictory – began to trickle in to Binche, Braine-le-Comté, Brussels. Napoleon was reported to be here, there and everywhere. A French deserter announced that the attack was planned for the following day.

They were, in fact, very close at hand.

According to the marching order drawn up by the Emperor and signed by him at Beaumont in the small hours of the

British Horse Artillery. After a painting by W. B. Wollen.

15th, the French Army was to march towards the Sambre in two groups of three columns.

The route stages were long. The men had to carry bread rations to last four days: the infantry of the 1st Corps, for lack of transportation, had to carry their own cartridges. The terrain was difficult, wooded: the valleys were narrow and deep; there were no roads – only country lanes, in bad condition, and footpaths. The heat was overpowering. It was only to be expected that there would be congestion and obstacles to be overcome along the way.

1st Group
Centre: 3rd Corps: General Vandamme, preceded by the cavalry under Domon and Pajol. 16,000 infantry, 2,400 cavalry. 50 guns. Line of march: Beaumont-Charleroi.
Left flank: 2nd Corps: General Reille. 25,000 men, 46 guns. Line of march: Solre-sur-Sambre, Thuin, Marchienne.
Right flank: 4th Corps: General Gérard. 15,800 men, 38 guns. Line of march: Florennes, Gerpinnes, Charleroi.

2nd Group
Centre: the Guard. 20,000 men, 126 guns. 6th Corps: General Mouton. 10,300 men, 32 guns.
Left flank: 1st Corps: General Drouet d'Erlon. 20,000 men, 46 guns. The order did not specify whether the corps was to cross the Sambre at Marchienne or at Charleroi.
Right flank: 14th Cavalry Division: General Delort. 1,600 cuirassiers, 6 guns.

A fourth line of march was reserved for Grouchy's cavalry – Beaumont-Yves-Tingremont-Charleroi – so as not to impede the infantry columns.

Napoleon had calculated the striking of the camps at half-hourly intervals to ensure that the units would be able to move ahead without impediment. The first were scheduled to cross the Sambre at 3 a.m., the last at 8 a.m. The French Army would be on the further bank before midday.

The order for this was lengthy, verbose and cluttered with detail that created misunderstanding. It resulted in making the crossing of the river difficult: four army corps and eight cavalry divisions had at their disposal only one bridge that could be easily defended and three equipment bridges in the train – if they could be constructed.

This was not an army of clean-shaven infantrymen, turned out in regulation dress, marching briskly in column of four and covering five kilometres an hour on a good road. It was an army corps column made up of a miscellany of infantry, cavalry, artillery, limbers, general service and kit waggons, lame horses, stragglers, cantinieres, camp-followers, carts: a world on the move.

Young and old, not properly trained, dirty, unkempt beards, faces drawn with hunger and fatigue, spattered with mud, heavily laden, carrying packs that swung as they marched, floundering through the ruts in batches of three, six, ten; tired horses, short of fodder; tricky moments for artillery-drivers and gunners when teams became bogged down in the mud.

All the endless walking, delayed by the crossing of a bridge in single file; by the hacking of a path through the thicket; by allowing men and animals time to get their breath; searching for a ford; waiting for an order or the termination of palavers and arguments about the road, path or short-cut to be taken . . . Vandamme's Corps formed a column $6\frac{1}{2}$ kilometres in depth, and if his marching speed had attained $2\frac{1}{2}$ kilometres an hour it would have been magnificent – sufficient to moderate the criticisms of certain intolerant historians. In this way the "French torrent" risked slowly draining itself even without the intervention of the Prussians.

In fact, the attack took place before Charleroi – not at the end of the British and Prussian sectors, which would have been a wasted effort, but to the right of the Prussian front held by von Ziethen's 1st Corps. His 2nd Brigade (Pirch II) provided the outposts between Thuin and Le Châtelet, with spearheads thrusting towards Ham-sur-Heure and Gerpinnes. The 3rd Brigade (von Jagow) was behind the Sambre; the 4th (von Henckel) was to the left of the 2nd, extending up to Namur. The 1st (von Steinmetz) guarded the frontier to the west of Charleroi and linked up at Binche with the Anglo-Netherlands army, the cavalry of which had not been put on the alert.

Napoleon at Charleroi. Lithograph, after Horace Vernet.

3. 15th June 1815

The French offensive

15th June. At the specified hour, drums and trumpets sounded reveille and boots-and-saddles – except for the 3rd Corps. In front of their companies, assistant quartermaster-sergeants read out the Emperor's proclamation, signed at Avesnes on the previous morning: "Soldiers, today is the anniversary of Marengo and Friedland: victory will be ours . . . For all true Frenchmen the time has come to conquer or to perish . . . "

This peroration was greeted with shouts of "Long live the Emperor!". The head of the centre column set off; but the 3rd Corps was still asleep in the morning mist when the 6th, which should have been following it, rushed into its bivouacs. Vandamme had received no marching orders. It was alleged that the orderly bringing them had broken his leg. In the past, Berthier had sent important orders in duplicate, triplicate or even quadruplicate by different messengers; but unfortunately, Berthier was dead . . .

A bad sleeper but a brave soldier, the commander of the 3rd Corps angrily rejected the admonishments of his opposite numbers and alerted his regiments – but 18,000 men were three hours behind schedule. The Guard and the pontoneers cursed. General Rogniat and General Haxo who, with the sappers and the marines of the Guard, should have marched behind Vandamme's first regiment went ahead of them after a heated exchange.

The Emperor was not aware of this set-back. Leaving Beaumont before daybreak with his staff and duty squadrons, he probably took the Barbençon road. In the woods at Gaiolet, Pajol's bivouacs were deserted; at Bossu-lez-Walcourt, Exelmans' dragoons were watering their horses. Marshal Grouchy was en route with the 1st Cavalry Corps. At Thy-le-Château, Napoleon crossed the frontier and alighted.

Biot, Pajol's aide-de-camp, was with his hussars in the square in front of the church, talking to a local inhabitant. He at once informed the Emperor that he was carrying out reconnaissance operations "to the right". The cavalry corps had struck camp at 3 a.m. to march on Charleroi. Roads had been cut by trenches and barred with fallen trees to make them unusable; work must have gone on throughout the night to block them. General Domon was reconnoitring ahead and to the left; he had made contact with the enemy towards Ham-sur-Heure, cut down some Prussians dressed in white – with French shakos on their heads – and some Landwehr men in tattered blue uniforms. Le Châtelet seemed to be held by only one brigade. The Staff of the 1st Prussian Corps was at Charleroi. No cavalry had been encountered.

Lieutenant-General Bourmont, 1773–1846, commander of the 14th Infantry Division (4th Corps). He deserted from the French Army on the morning of 15th June. Engraving by Julien, after Nordheim. Musée Royal de l'Armée, Brussels.

15th June 1815 at 11 a.m. The marines and sappers of the Guard clear the Charleroi bridge. Illustration by Jean Augé, from Le Champ de Bataille de Waterloo, *Éditions Baudart*

From elsewhere the march was slow: it was difficult to see through the mist that clung to the shallows and blurred the outlines of the woods. Then the sun swept the mist away: it was going to be hot.

The Emperor remounted, cantered towards Jamioulx and stopped in a field near the vicarage. The curé was amiable: a snack, a glass of good red wine, plans for the future. If everything went well, the Abbé Jénicot would be made a bishop. (Was it true that, as a souvenir of the Imperial promise, his parishioners later gave him a bishop's crook?)

General Rogniat arrived. Probably notified by him of Vandamme's delay, Napoleon sent for the Guard. It would head the centre column . . . a verbal order, perhaps . . .

Then he ordered the Chief of Staff to write to Reille and d'Erlon as follows:

Order to Reille to cross the Sambre. If there are no forces opposing him, he is to form up along several lines one or two leagues ahead in such a way as to be mounted on the main

Major-General Count von Tippelskirch, commander of the 5th Brigade of the 2nd Prussian Corps. Artist unknown. Musée Royal de l'Armée, Brussels.

65

General Pajol's cavalry, backed by the sappers and marines of the Guard, take the Charleroi bridge.

Château Puissant at Charleroi.

Brussels road in reconnoitring in strength in the direction of Fleurus.

The order ended thus:

The Comte d'Erlon will cross at Marchienne and take up battle stations along the road from Mons to Charleroi so that he will be at hand to give you any assistance required. Should you still be at Marchienne when the present order reaches you and the movement through Charleroi is not able to take place, you will still go via Marchienne but still with the intention of carrying out the above dispositions. The Emperor is proceeding to Charleroi. Report on your operations.

What gibberish! The order was not clear. And the one to d'Erlon was even less so:

The Emperor has instructed me to inform you that the Comte de Reille has been ordered to cross the Sambre at Charleroi and form up on several lines one or two leagues ahead and to occupy the main Brussels road with mounted troops.

The intention of His Majesty is that you should cross the Sambre at Marchienne or at Ham in order to bring you to the main road from Mons to Charleroi, where you will form up on several lines and take positions that will bring you nearer to the directions of Mons-Nivelles, etc. This movement should be executed even if the Comte de Reille is obliged to make the crossing at Marchienne.

What was the Commandant of the 1st Corps to make of all this? Ham-sur-Sambre did not exist. Nor did the Mons-Charleroi road. Soult had just ordered Reille to cross the Sambre at Marchienne "if he could" and had told d'Erlon that the 2nd Corps would cross the river at Charleroi.

Soult could neither interpret the Emperor's thoughts nor draft an order. His staff did not know the rudiments of their job. Berthier's officers – drunkards, gamblers, breakers of hearts – were never put off by any obstacle, be it a river or a marshal: but they were no more.

8.30 a.m. Reille marched on Marchienne and did not care to risk the crossing at Charleroi, which was extremely congested. At noon, the 2nd Light overthrew the Prussian battalion that was defending the bridge (Solre-sur-Sambre was 28 kilometres from Marchienne).

In the column on the right, one could already count several traitors. General Bourmont, commanding the 14th Division (4th Corps), deserted with his staff on the morning of the battle, thereby dishonouring his name. There followed great disturbance among the regiments. Much time was lost in restoring order: but Gérard finally managed to reassure the troops, who spat out the name of the traitor between an oath and a curse and wanted only to advance against the enemy.

The Dowager Puissant d'Hensy, who received Napoleon at Charleroi. Collection of the Chevalier Puissant d'Agimont, Brussels.

Charleroi

At Charleroi the enemy was in full retreat. Domon's cavalry had been at their heels since the early hours of the morning. Dommanget's brigade had overthrown some companies of the 9th Prussians outside Couillet and had occupied Marcinelle; but when they encountered resistance on the dyke leading towards Charleroi, the chasseurs were repulsed. The bridge was protected by a palisade, barricaded and defended in front and in the rear. It was therefore necessary to wait until the infantry arrived (along the Beaumont-Charleroi roads – 32 kilometres).

Early in the afternoon of 15th June, Napoleon was given a frenzied ovation by the troops, who filed past the Belle-vue tavern. Behind the Emperor: Marshal Soult, General de la Bédoyère and an officer of the 5th Hussars. Drawing by James Thiriar, Musée Royal de l'Armée, Brussels.

Charleroi was strongly fortified – and since Lasalle's death the light cavalry no longer attacked fortified towns. This one, in 1815, was built along both banks of the Sambre. The lower part of the town, on the right bank, was connected to the village of Marcinelle by a dyke some four hundred metres long and bordered by hedges. Thanks to this, there was a flooded region to cross; then, by means of a lane leading off at right-angles, access was gained to a square planted with trees – later to be known as the Place du Sud – to which led the one and only bridge across the Sambre. The bridge was hog-backed and measured only eight metres wide between its wooden parapets. Beyond the bridge, a street – now called rue de la Montagne – climbed towards the upper town, which was built in the shape of an amphitheatre on a hill. First one came to the Place du Centre and then to the crossroads formed by the Brussels and Flerus roads, a short distance from the ruins of the ramparts near the Belle-Vue tavern. The slopes were cluttered with houses and gardens; there were a number of coalpits in the district.

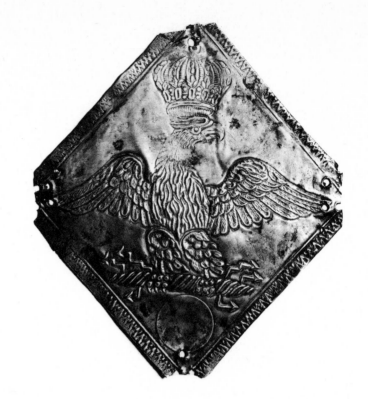

On 15th June, two battalions of the 6th Prussians (Pirch II Brigade) occupied Charleroi. Ziethen had established his headquarters there that morning. Alerted in good time by Reille's cannon from the direction of Maladrie, near Thuin, the Prussian general had ordered warning salvoes to be fired, informing both Blücher and Wellington: "I am withdrawing everybody to Charleroi." He was already there when Steinmetz, forewarned of the French attack by his outposts, which the 2nd French Corps had successfully dislodged, endeavoured to recall his scattered forces. Steinmetz then warned his neighbour on his right – General van Merlen, who was installed at Saint-Symphorien (Wellington's army) – and withdrew at about 10 o'clock to Gosselies.

From 8 o'clock Ziethen had been moving his 2nd Brigade back to Gilly; at 1 o'clock Pirch II had occupied the woods in front of Flerus. There had been no French unit to impede his troops during this operation.

It was, in fact, only about 12.30 p.m. when Rogniat's sappers and the marines of the Guard attacked the Charleroi bridge and threw the barricades into the Sambre. The Emperor, who had been waiting for this since 11 a.m., immediately launched Pajol's cavalry. General Ameil, at the head of his hussars, was seen trotting briskly up rue de la Montagne and disappearing into the outskirts of Gilly. But on entering, a volley of grape shot forced him to halt his regiments and prepare to repulse a possible Prussian attack. The sappers and the marines went on, followed by the Young Guard.

Pajol sent the squadrons into Gilly and Colonel Clary, with the 1st Hussars, along the road to Brussels.

The Emperor set up his headquarters in the lower part of the town in a mansion belonging to the local ironmaster, M. Puissant, where he had the lunch that had been prepared for Ziethen.

An hour later, when Napoleon entered Charleroi to the acclamation of a section of the local population, the situation was as follows:

To the left, one – possibly two – of Reille's divisions had crossed the Sambre.

In the centre, the Young Guard was leaving Marcinelle, followed by the dragoons under Exelmans. The light cavalry of the Guard (Lefebvre-Desnoëttes), called up by the Emperor, had overtaken the infantry columns and was approaching from Marcinelle. Chasseurs and lancers dismounted to water their horses, and they crossed the bridge ahead of the dragoons.

The 3rd Corps was still a long way off: the cuirassiers and the convoys continued to lag and would not cross the Sambre that day.

To the right, Hulot's division (ex-Bourmont) crossed the frontier.

The first geographical objective had been taken, but the Prussians had disappeared almost without a fight and were still free to operate.

Napoleon had planned to have 60,000 men and 134 guns beyond the Sambre by noon; but, at most, 20,000 men had made the crossing.

If he gave any orders between noon and 2 p.m., no record of them has yet been found.

There is a picture of him in front of the Belle-Vue tavern, sitting astride a chair, rather drowsy despite the cheers of the Young Guard marching past. Behind him is the guide from Charleroi, Germain Thévenier, who accompanied him as far as Fleurus.

The Emperor was tired.

Information was coming in. His senior personal staff officer Gourgaud, who had been sent out along the Brussels road, reported contacts between the 1st Hussars and the uhlans near Jumet; some Prussian infantry was at Gosselies. It was the 29th Prussian Regiment, sent by Ziethen to protect the flank march by Steinmetz from Fontaine-l'Evêque, at the moment passing Piéton and advancing over difficult terrain towards Gosselies in order to reach Heppignies and Fleurus. The uhlans were endeavouring to draw the hussars off, but

Colonel Clary did not understand anything about what was happening.

Badly informed, the Emperor despatched a regiment of the Young Guard towards Lodelinsart in support of the 1st Hussars and directed the rest towards Gilly. The entire Guard was soon mustered near the crossroads, where they waited with their arms at the order. Pajol, however, due to the foundering of a large number of his horses, signalled that he was held up in front of the Fleurus woods by Prussian infantry and cannon. Were the Prussians everywhere, then? On the road to Brussels as well as on the road to Fleurus?

Lieutenant-General Habert, commander of the 10th Infantry Division of the 3rd Corps. Musée de l'Armée, Paris.

The Prussians retreat

3 p.m. Napoleon gave orders:

– to Reille, to march on Gosselies and attack the enemy who seemed to have halted there;

– to d'Erlon, to follow Reille – "Back him up in his operations"; to guard Marchienne; and to despatch "along the Mons roads a brigade capable, in the military sense, of taking care of itself";

– to Gérard, to cross the Sambre – not at Charleroi, where there was heavy congestion, but at Le Châtelet.

These orders do not reveal any intention of attacking the enemy. Moreover, the operations specified were difficult to execute.

On the map, it was 9 kilometres from Marchienne to Gosselies going through the heart of Piéton and the woods. It would therefore take the 2nd Corps, with a column measuring 7½ kilometres, at least three hours . . . Thus only its cavalry, led by General Piré, and possibly half of Bachelu's division would be capable of stepping in to gather together the 1st Hussars, who were extremely tired, and to push Steinmetz on his way to Fleurus. As for d'Erlon, his first units were still on the right bank of the Sambre, the approaches to which were littered with the waggons of the 2nd Corps.

And from these inevitable delays the Prussians profited.

Two-thirds of the 1st Corps were in retreat towards Fleurus. Ziethen had no difficulty in carrying out Blücher's order: fall back as slowly as possible and protect the army concentrated at Sombreffe. Only Steinmetz's brigade might have been in danger; but no serious French attack developed.

However, Blücher feared that one might be launched. If Napoleon – whose methods he knew extremely well – pursued the 1st Corps vigorously, he would have to retreat to avoid having his three army corps destroyed in succession, for the concentration of his forces at Sombreffe could not be terminated before 4 p.m. By that time . . .

But Blücher acted as if he were completely alone. There was no attempt at planning in concert with Wellington. And Gneisenau had no confidence in the Duke and did not request an exchange of views with him.

Directly, while at table with the Prince of Orange, the Duke read the despatches . . . The French had attacked the Prussians in front of Charleroi. The British sector was quiet . . . Perhaps that was a feint. In any event, it was the main thing for the moment. This business was Blücher's concern.

At Braine-le-Comte, General de Constant Rebecque was less convinced. Since 9th June he had kept his divisions on the alert and increased the orders to be carried out in the event of an attack. Warned at 10.30 a.m., he reinforced with one brigade the few Nassau battalions holding Quatre-Bras and prepared marching orders for sending two divisions to this point. As a matter of fact, his leaders wanted to defend Brussels, the main road to which was open to the French. Major Normann noted that the peasants were fleeing before the soldiers to announce their pending arrival at Charleroi, where Napoleon had made his entry at noon at the head of the Imperial Guard.

Since 4 p.m. gunfire had been heard from the direction of Gosselies.

It was coming from the forces of Marshal Ney, who had arrived at Belle-Vue at about 3.30 p.m. He had come from Paris, probably via Mézières since the Prefect spoke of having a guest for supper to whom he had sold two horses – certainly not Beaumont or Marshal Mortier, who was riveted to his bed by an attack of gout. Skirting round the troop columns, the Prince of the Moscova rejoined Napoleon.

What did Napoleon say to him? Did he order him to occupy the crossroads at Quatre-Bras? There were no witnesses: the officers present were too far away to overhear the conversation. And who would have been bold enough to approach without being summoned? Historians find themselves faced with the biased account of events resulting from the subsequent conversations at St. Helena.

In a letter to Fouché, however, the Marshal wrote:

I arrived at Charleroi on the 15th at the time when the enemy, attacked by our light troops, was withdrawing to Fleurus and Gosselies. The Emperor ordered me to immediately put myself at the head of the 1st and 2nd Infantry Corps, of General Piré's cavalry division, a division of light cavalry of the Guard, and two divisions under Count Valmy. With these troops I pursued the enemy and forced them to evacuate Gosselies, Frasnes, Mellet and Heppignies: there, they took up their position.

His report from Gosselies at 11 p.m. contained the following reference:

In conformity with the Emperor's orders, I went to Gosselies this afternoon to dislodge the enemy who had fallen back on Fleurus by way of Heppignies.

There was no mention of Quatre-Bras.

Had the Emperor wished to occupy the crossroads in the afternoon of 15th June he would at least have mentioned it to Reille, to whom he had ordered a communication to be sent just before the fortuitous arrival of the Marshal.

Furthermore, what could he know of the significance of Quatre-Bras? When he crossed into Belgium on 15th June there was heavy mist everywhere. He knew that Wellington was in Brussels and that Blücher was in Namur. It would have been impossible for him to make an accurate assessment of the situation.

The Emperor was a great man, but he was not able to read the future or make forecasts without accurate intelligence reports concerning the enemy's positions and intentions. He was gifted with very keen observation, and his deductions were rapid and logical although sometimes exaggerated by his imagination. His decisions were instantaneous. But when he did not know what was going on he would walk about, hands behind his back, or sleep while awaiting information. Significantly – and this is where he showed his superiority over so many others – he needed only a small amount of information on which to act.

As for Marshal Ney, when he left at about 5 p.m. to overtake the light division of the Guard (Lefebvre-Desnoëttes) that had been placed under his command – a command he had no authority to use – he knew no more of the Emperor's intentions than that he had to march against the Prussians.

Sombreffe. The Rectory. Blücher's headquarters on 15th June 1815.

General Count Letort, 1773–1815, aide-de-camp to the Emperor, commander of the dragoons of the Guard. He was mortally wounded in combat at Gilly. Collection d'Harville.

LE GÉNÉRAL COMTE LETORT
AIDE DE CAMP DE L'EMPEREUR
NAPOLÉON 1ER
EST MORT DANS CETTE MAISON
LE 16 JUIN 1815.

CERCLE NAPOLÉON

Death of General Letort. Collection of J. Hagon-Jumet.

72

The battle of Gilly

This is where Grouchy was, having arrived with Pajol. Exelmans and his dragoons were also at Gilly. About 20,000 Prussians occupied the Fleurus woods up to the Sambre as well as the Abbey of Soleilmont and Pironchamp. The small stream at Gilly acted as a moat to their position. The road to Fleurus was blocked by felled trees, and there were troops between this village and Lambusart. Pajol's cavalry was in contact with the enemy; the artillery battle had begun. The Emperor, wanting to find out for himself what the situation was, spurred his horse towards Gilly.

The reconnaissance completed, he issued his orders.

The Prussians did not number more than 10,000. Infantry and artillery would be needed to dislodge them. This would be the task of the 3rd Corps. As soon as Vandamme arrived, Marshal Grouchy would attack the Prussians on the right and drive them back towards Fleurus and Sombreffe.

These instructions must have been given verbally, for no written order has ever been found.

Napoleon decided to make use of the Guard, which had been mustered for some time near the crossroads, since time was pressing. He set off to get in front of Vandamme and let him know what was expected of him.

Watch in hand, Grouchy was growing impatient. Time was passing. What if the Prussians should attack?

They had no such intention.

The Marshal was confronted by Pirch II's brigade: 7 battalions, 8 guns – 6,500 men who had escaped from Charleroi, including some cavalry; the remainder had been wiped out. The position they now occupied, carefully studied since May by Ziethen's general staff, dominated the gorges of Charleroi and Le Châtelet. Taking advantage of the Fleurus woods, Pirch could disappear without risk of pursuit; but he had only a few meagre battalions with which to hold the position until nightfall.

His superior officer had, in fact, been ordered by Blücher not to fall back beyond Fleurus since it was Blücher's intention to concentrate the whole army at Sombreffe on the following day. Like the infantry under Steinmetz, which had now reached Heppignies and Wangenies declaring that it was worn out, Pirch was prepared to fight to the death if the French attacked.

But the French did not attack: their artillery merely fired a few cannonballs from time to time.

Gilly, 5 p.m. The heads of the columns of the 3rd Corps spilled on to the plateau. Vandamme had safely received the Emperor's order to attack the Prussians and drive them back

Major-General von Jagow, commander of the 3rd Brigade of the 1st Corps.

Lieutenant-General Baron Burthe, 1772–1830, commander of the 5th and 13th Dragoons of the 2nd Cavalry Corps.

to Fleurus but not the one to obey Grouchy's orders, and Vandamme was therefore disagreeable. A good hour was taken up in unpleasant discussions, and the soldiers rested.

The Emperor was furious when he did not hear the expected cannon. He immediately assumed command: Major Doguereau's artillery at the centre; the infantry, deployed in three columns, to attack the Abbey of Soleilmont; Grouchy, with Exelmans' division, to intervene on the right flank and press beyond the woods. Pajol would be in reserve.

The attack began at 6 p.m. Pirch, overwhelmed, quickly gave the order to retreat on Lambusart and Fleurus; and Napoleon, exasperated because the Prussians were once again escaping, launched the duty squadrons led by his aide-de-camp Letort on the heels of the 6th Prussian Regiment. Two squares were swept away to shouts of "Long live the Emperor", but Letort was mortally wounded. Pajol pursued the enemy as far as Lambusart.

Napoleon, very tired, returned to Charleroi after ordering Grouchy to take Fleurus and push on to Sombreffe. But the soldiers of the 3rd Corps were exhausted by a tiring march of 40 kilometres in intense heat: and Vandamme refused to give the Marshal even one battalion despite the insistence of Exelmans and Pajol.

Evening fell and the battle ended. Waggons loaded with the wounded made their way along the road. "Keep on, comrades," one of them called. "Everything is going well. A bit more courage and they will flee." One of the dying added, "Long live the Emperor! Damnation to the Prussians!"

Pirch II had reached Fleurus: Hulot's division had crossed the Sambre at Le Châtelet . . . too late to cut off his retreat.

Why had the Emperor waited from 2 p.m. until 6 p.m. to attack the Prussians at Gilly?

Inactivity of the British army

Mystery, too, on the road to Brussels.

At about 4 p.m., with Bachelu's division of the 2nd Corps, Marshal Ney had repulsed a Prussian attack launched on Gosselies by Steinmetz, to give himself a breathing space, and had caused the Prussians to be pursued along the road to Fleurus by Girard's division (2nd Corps). The latter stopped at Wangenies.

Lefebvre-Desnoëttes' division, despatched against Frasnes at about 6.30 p.m., was received with musket-fire. Before the manoeuvres of the French lancers, the enemy fell back on Quatre-Bras.

Which enemy?

It was not the Prussians: the infantry were clothed in green: some wore a busby. These were the troops alerted at about noon by the exodus of the country folk. Major Normann, of Nassau-Usingen, had warned Colonel Prince Bernard of Saxe-Weimar at Genappe and General Perponcher at Nivelles. Shortly afterwards a few battalions had arrived, led by the Prince. The crossroads and neighbouring vantage points were occupied by five battalions of Nassau or Orange Nassau and eight guns. In the Fleurus direction, the cannon roared. Two items of information help to clarify the position in this sector: Frasnes, 15th June, 9 p.m. General Lefebvre-Desnoëttes to Marshal Ney:

Wellington's hat, preserved at the National Army Museum.

The troops that we found at Frasnes had not been fighting at Gosselies; they were under the Duke of Wellington's orders. None of the troops that had been fighting at Gosselies this morning passed this way. They went on to Fleurus. Tomorrow, at daybreak, I will send out a reconnaissance party to Quatre-Bras which will, if possible, occupy this position, because I believe the Nassau troops have gone . . .

At the same time, Prince Bernard, Commander of the 2nd Brigade of Perponcher's division, was writing from Quatre-Bras to his chief, who was at Nivelles:

At about 6.30 p.m. the enemy attacked the forward posts at Frasnes with infantry and artillery; the Nassau battalion and the battery still there withdrew half way to Quatre-Bras. During this time, the brigade reassembled at Quatre-Bras. One battalion was posted near Frasnes, another near Houtain-le-Val.

The infantry and artillery referred to were a battalion of the 2nd Corps and the horse-drawn battery of Lefebvre-Desnoëttes. One can only pay tribute to the way the leaders of the Netherlands army took action.

At about 11 p.m. the situation would appear to have been as follows:

The Emperor and his Imperial Headquarters were at the 'Palace' – that is, the mansion belonging to the Puissant family.

General Baron von Müffling, Prussian liaison officer at the British headquarters. Reproduced from a colour photograph in the Musée Royal de l'Armée, Brussels. Original in the collection of Baron von Müffling, Loizenkirchen, Bavaria.

Grouchy's group was to the right, on the line Charleroi-Fleurus: Pajol at Lambusart, on horseback and on the Fleurus road; Grouchy and Exelmans at Campinaire; Vandamme at the Fontenelle farm, in the woods; the Guard between Gilly and Charleroi; the Hulot Division (4th Corps) in front of Le Châtelet.

Ney's group was to the left, on the line Charleroi-Brussels. The Marshal lodged with M. Dumont in the rue Saint-Roch. Lefebvre-Desnoëttes' division was at Frasnes; Bachelu's division (2nd Corps) was at Mellet-Frasnes; General Reille and Foy's division (2nd Corps) were at Gosselies; Girard's division was at Wangenies; Jérôme Napoléon's division was at Ransart; Piré's cavalry was at Heppignies. Count d'Erlon was at Jumet, but his divisions were to the rear; Quoit was at Thuin; half the cavalry was at Solre-sur-Sambre; Marcognet was at Marchienne; Donzelot, Durutte and half Jacquinot's cavalry were around Jumet. On the right bank of the Sambre were the 4th Corps (except for Hulot's division), the 6th Corps near Bomerée, and the cuirassiers, the convoys, etc. to the rear.

It was a hot night, and there was a full moon to light up the camps.

Ziethen's forces were bivouacking at Fleurus. A despatch from Blücher announced his arrival, with the 2nd Corps under Pirch I, at Sombreffe at about noon on the following day. The 3rd Corps (von Thielmann) would be at Mazy and the 4th Corps (von Bülow) near Gembloux. In consequence, the 1st Corps would have to hold out where it was until it was destroyed.

Twelve hours of anguish. It was feared that Napoleon would launch a surprise attack at daybreak on 16th June, when the sun rose at 3.48 a.m.

Unless Wellington took the offensive . . .

Major-General von Pirch I, commander of the 2nd Corps, Army of the Lower Rhine.

The Duchess of Richmond's Ball

The Duke of Richmond. After a portrait by Hoppner.

The Duke of Wellington in full dress uniform.

The Duchess of Richmond gives a ball for Wellington, who has been secretly informed by Blücher of the capture of Charleroi.

Hotel de Richmond, Brussels.

Wellington was at the ball given by the Duke and Duchess of Richmond. Furthermore, there had been no excitement in Brussels during the day of the 15th; nor had there been any agitation among the General Staffs. All had gone about their usual business: walks; letters home; skimming through despatches from the front, which had been more or less identical for the past four days.

6 p.m. General von Müffling called on the Duke. He bore a letter from Gneisenau, despatched from Namur at noon: a major attack by the French. Blücher was mustering his corps at Sombreffe.

7 p.m. In a 'movement order', Wellington stationed his divisions on the roads leading from the frontier to Brussels. He drafted a plan whereby the Netherlands forces would be concentrated at Nivelles and his British troops would be retained on his right flank to oppose any movement by Napoleon that might threaten his communication with Ostend, the sea and his ships.

Had this order been executed by General de Constant, he would have evacuated Quatre-Bras. But the Chief of the Netherlands General Staff thought the matter over: Blücher at Sombreffe, the Prince of Orange at Nivelles . . . the road to

Brussels, which the Duke wanted to defend, would be left open if he did not hold on to Quatre-Bras.

10 p.m. A despatch from General von Dörnberg, containing news of events at the frontiers, that had left Mons at 9.30 a.m. . . . 55 kilometres in twelve hours. Wellington was right: the General Staffs were not doing their job properly.

New orders were drawn up: the slipping of the Army of the Low Countries to the left had to begin that night. Müffling hurried this good news to Namur. But the General Staff did not even know how to reproduce the orders, of which some copies were incomprehensible.

It was now time to go to the ball in order to give confidence to the citizens of Brussels. Generals and officers who had been invited made their way there. But – could it have been an oversight? – General von Müffling was not among the guests.

Supper was served at 11.30 p.m. It was a magnificent night, and the party was elegant and gay. A few non-commissioned officers and pipers of the Gordon Highlanders performed some Scottish dances in the garden: the sword-dance, some reels . . .

11.40 p.m. Lieutenant Webster arrived from Braine-le-Comte (30 kilometres in one hour and three-quarters). He had a communication from General de Constant: the enemy was approaching Quatre-Bras. The general had taken it upon himself to move Perponcher's division towards the crossroads, alerting Chassé's division to be ready to support it.

Wellington advanced by two hours the departure to Quatre-Bras of the British garrison in Brussels, reassured the dancers and then discreetly withdrew; his officers took . . . French leave. Outside, the drums beat the call to arms into the night.

In the 'Imperial Palace of Charleroi', the Emperor, very tired, was still asleep. In the courtyard, the 2nd Battalion of the 1st Grenadiers was on duty: arms were piled, weapons were cleaned, leather equipment was polished. Posts, sentries and patrols operated as if it were the Elysée. Inside, in the beautiful apartments belonging to the ironmaster Puissant, Soult's general staff was at work. The First Secretary, Baron Fain, was writing to Prince Joseph:

Charleroi, 15 June 1815, 9 p.m.

The Emperor, who was on horseback from 3 a.m., came back exhausted. He threw himself on to his bed to get a few hours' rest. He has to remount at midnight. Not being able to do so himself, His Majesty has instructed me to write to Your Royal Highness as follows: The Army has forced a passage across the Sambre near Charleroi and posted advance guards half way between Charleroi and Namur, and Charleroi and Brussels. We have taken 1,500 prisoners and 6 cannons. Four Prussian regiments have been crushed. The Emperor has lost very few men, but he has sustained one particularly severe loss: that is his aide-de-camp, General Letort, who was killed in action on the Fleurus plateau while leading a cavalry charge. The enthusiasm of the local inhabitants is beyond description. It is possible that there will be a major battle tomorrow.

This was not quite accurate. Four Prussian regiments had not been crushed. Above all, Lambusart was 10 kilometres from Charleroi and 22 from Namur; Frasnes was 14 kilometres from Charleroi and 38 from Brussels. And no one really thought that the Emperor would leave at midnight . . .

That document was just as erroneous as the army bulletins sent off during the evening. In those days there was a saying – "lying like a bulletin". It was what governments called "not alarming the public".

In fact, during the evening of the first day the offensive resulted in an advance of two leagues towards Fleurus. Two brigades of the 1st Prussian Corps lost 2,000 men and fell back on the two others installed at Fleurus. The anticipated battle did not take place.

The Emperor thought that Blücher, who had been strongly affected by the sudden appearance of the French near his dispersed forces, would beat a retreat. Consequently, Grouchy would advance on Sombreffe early next morning.

He also considered that the attacks engaged in by Ney were of secondary importance: they were a question of a simple show of force against the English. The Prussians were in retreat. Wellington would not be able to withstand a French attack unaided and would probably fall back . . . In any event, with his forces scattered, the Duke would not be able to intervene before the 17th . . . The Prince of Moscova had sufficient troops at his command to overthrow any enemy troops that presented themselves . . . This would then turn into "the clash with the English" predicted before Napoleon left Paris.

. . . Unless Reille was right. "It might", he had said, "turn out to be a type of 'Spanish battle' in which the English appear only when the time is ripe."

In war, certainly, anything could happen.

But Napoleon underestimated his opponents and entertained some strange illusions. How could he have imagined that old 'Vorwärts', who was fighting mad, and the Duke of Wellington, who exemplified British tenacity, would give up the struggle without so much as firing a gun?

In the early morning, the English officers leave the ball. After a painting by Hillingford.

Led by their officers, the 92nd Gordon Highlanders leave Brussels early in the morning.

From Wellington's hand the Duke of Brunswick receives Blücher's letter confirming the French invasion of Belgium.

Colonel Sir William Home de Lancey, Quartermaster-General of the Army of the Low Countries, who was mortally wounded on 18th June. After a painting in the possession of his family.

4. 16th June 1815

The battle of Ligny

Charleroi owes its name to Charles II of Spain. Its inhabitants live on a battlefield between Mons and Namur, and for several centuries they have known what it is to be in the midst of war, sieges, capitulation and marches of triumphal entry. At that time they readily acclaimed Napoleon; but they feared his soldiers, who had a reputation as pillagers and whose lack of discipline was well known. They preferred the English, who were governed by an iron fist and who paid well. However, everything is relative: they were prepared to welcome the French because they had chased away the Prussians – brutal, mean, ravenous and hating anyone who spoke French.

The grenadiers on duty at the 'Palace' prepared food for that day and the next; the previous day they had not unhooked their dixies for as long as sixteen hours and had been predicting that there would be a battle on the 16th. At midnight

Panorama of the Ligny battlefield. In the foreground, General Vandamme's infantry are preparing to attack the village.

The Battle of Ligny, 16th June 1815. Napoleon, at the foot of the Fleurus windmill, giving orders for the attack. Engraving by Philippoteaux. This print makes it clear that Saint-Amand was very near Napoleon's observation post and that Ligny, on the contrary, was far away.

on the 15th the cavalry took over. In the town, near the bridge, there was a massive pile-up of vehicles and disorder among the laggards that General Radet's military police and Captain Coignet's oaths were unable to overcome.

The Emperor rose at 4 a.m. After reading the latest reports, he saw no need to change his assessment of the situation: his army, now concentrated in a triangle measuring three leagues on each side, would drive Blücher back to Maestricht and Wellington to the sea . . .

Soult, summoned shortly afterwards, issued orders to Grouchy and to Ney. Grouchy was to move towards Sombreffe and take a position there: the 3rd and 4th Corps and the cavalry corps under Pajol, Exelmans and Milhaud were at his disposal. But "when His Majesty is present, the generals will receive their orders direct". Ney, with the 1st and 2nd Corps and Kellermann's cuirassiers, was to take position at Quatre-Bras and keep watch in the direction of Nivelles. He was to send a division and some cavalry to Genappe and a

The battle of Ligny

Blücher's Prussians were solidly entrenched in the villages bordering the small river of Ligny – more particularly at Saint-Amand and at Ligny.

Napoleon ordered Vandamme to attack Saint-Amand from west to east and Gérard to attack Ligny from south to north, restricting Grouchy to keeping the enemy's left flank under surveillance.

After waiting in vain for d'Erlon, recalled from Quatre-Bras, to break through and attack the Prussian right flank from the rear, the Emperor resolved to pierce the enemy centre of the western outskirts of Ligny by ordering up the Guard and Milhaud's cuirassiers. This forced Blücher to abandon the battlefield and fall back, under cover of darkness, to Gembloux.

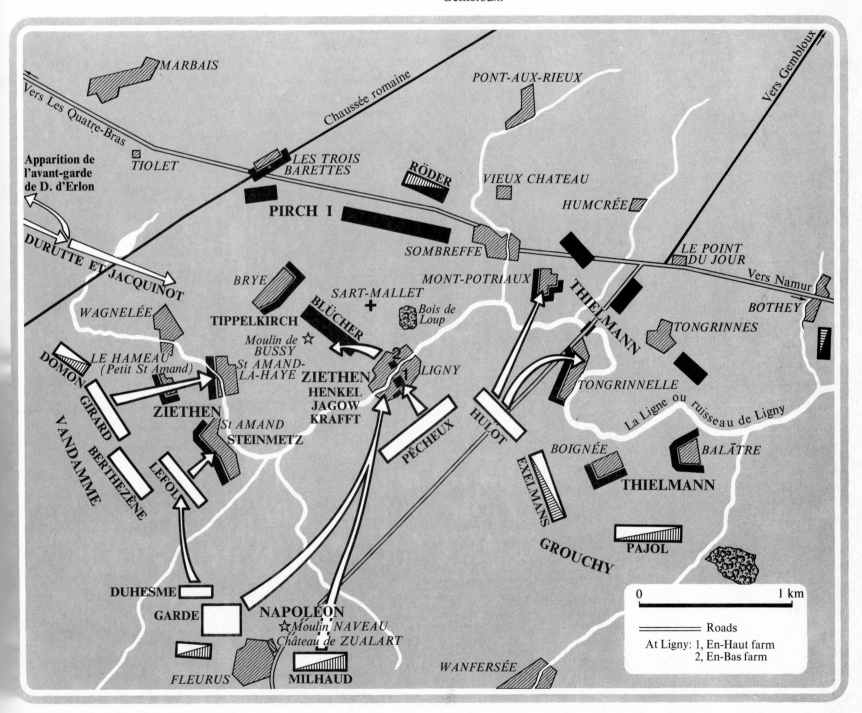

Lieutenant-General Count Vandamme, 1770–1830, commander of the 3rd Corps. After a portrait by Rouillard.

Lieutenant-General Count Gérard, 1773–1852, commander of the 4th Corps. Collection of Commandant Lachouque.

Stream at Ligny.

similar detachment to Marbais. Both were to reconnoitre – the former towards Brussels, the latter towards Gembloux-Wavre.

Then reports began to filter in.

Grouchy and Girard signalled at 5 a.m. that the Prussian columns were leaving Fleurus and moving in the direction of Brye and Saint-Amand; others had reached Point-du-Jour . . .

This information was confirmed at 6 a.m.

The Emperor pondered, hesitated, called for his aide-de-camp General Flahaut and, between 8.30 and 9 a.m., dictated to him the following order for Marshal Ney:

My cousin, I am sending my aide-de-camp Flahaut to you. The Chief of Staff will have sent you his orders, but you will receive mine first because my officers are better mounted and can move faster than his. You will receive the general marching order for the day, but I want to write to you in detail about it because it is of the greatest importance. I am sending Marshal Grouchy with the 3rd and 4th Infantry Corps against Sombreffe; I am sending my Guard against Fleurus; I will be there in person before noon. I will attack the enemy there if I encounter them, and I will reconnoitre the road to Gembloux. There, depending on what happens, I will make my decision, possibly at 3 p.m., possibly this evening. My intention is that, immediately after I have made my decision, you will be ready to march on Brussels.

I will give you support with the Guard, which will be at Fleurus or at Sombreffe, and I would like to arrive at Brussels tomorrow morning. You will start off this same evening, and if I reach a decision early enough for you to be informed today you can then advance this evening 3 or 4 leagues and be in Brussels at 7 o'clock in the morning.

You can therefore deploy your troops as follows: one division two leagues in front of Quatre-Bras, if there is nothing to prevent this; six divisions around Quatre-Bras and one division at Marbais, so that I can draw it to me at Sombreffe if I need it. This should not, however, delay your march. Count de Valmy's corps, consisting of 3,000 crack cuirassiers, will be stationed at the intersection of the Roman road and the main Brussels road so that I can draw on it if required. As soon as my decision has been taken, you will send him the order to rejoin you.

I would like to have near me the Guards divisions under General Lefebvre-Desnoëttes, and I am sending you two divisions of Count de Valmy's corps in replacement. But in my present plan, I prefer Count de Valmy to be available, should I need him, and not have to cause General Lefebvre-Desnoëttes to make a forced march, since it is probable that I will decide this evening to march on Brussels with the Guard. However, cover the division of Lefebvre-Desnoëttes with the two cavalry divisions under d'Erlon and Reille in order to spare the Guard; for if there is to be some clash with the English, it is better that it should be with the Line rather than with the Guard.

Ligny Church, which changed hands several times during the battle.

The general principle that I have adopted for this campaign is to divide my army into two flanks and a reserve. Your flank will consist of 4 divisions of the 1st Corps, 4 divisions of the 2nd Corps, two divisions of light cavalry, and the two divisions of Count de Valmy. This should not be far from 40,000 to 50,000 men. Marshal Grouchy will have about the same number of troops and will command the right flank. The Guard will form the reserve, and I will move on one flank or the other, according to circumstances.

The Chief of Staff will give strict instructions to ensure that no difficulties arise over your orders being obeyed after you have been detached; corps commanders will have to take orders direct from me when I am present.

Depending on events, I may have to weaken one or other flank to strengthen my reserves. You know full well how important it is to capture Brussels. That could give rise to incidents from another source since such a rapid and sudden movement would isolate the British Army from Mons and Ostend, and it is my wish that your arrangements are well made so that at the first order your eight

Battle of Ligny. Engraving attributed to G. Bottger, Senior. Published by Camp in 1816. Musée Royal de l'Armée, Brussels.

General Girard, commander of the 7th Infantry Division, who was created Duke of Ligny on the battlefield and was mortally wounded at about 4 p.m. Collection d'Harville.

Death of General Girard. Private collection.

divisions will be able to march rapidly and without hindrance on Brussels.

The order dictated to Baron Fain and taken to Grouchy by Napoleon's aide-de-camp General La Bédoyère was just as lengthy, a little simpler, but containing the same restrictions.

. . . on the right flank, the 3rd and 4th Corps, and the cavalry corps under Pajol, Exelmans and Milhaud will meet at Sombreffe.
I will arrive at Fleurus between 10 o'clock and 11 o'clock. I will proceed to Sombreffe, leaving the Guard at Fleurus; I will call the Guard to Sombreffe only if it should prove necessary. If the enemy are at Sombreffe, I want to attack them there; I also want to attack the enemy at Gembloux and take this position, my intention being, after I have occupied these two positions, to leave this same night and to move my left flank, under Marshal Ney's command, against the English. Do not waste a moment, because the sooner I make my decision the better it will be for the whole course of operations.
I assume that you are at Fleurus. Keep in constant touch with General Gérard so that he can assist you in attacking Sombreffe, if necessary. Girard's division is within reach of Fleurus: do not make use of it if you can avoid it since it will have to march throughout the night. Leave also my Young Guard and all its artillery at Fleurus. Count de Valmy, with his two cuirassier divisions, is marching on the road to Brussels; he is linking up with Marshal Ney to contribute to this evening's operation on the left flank. I will be at Fleurus between 10 and 11 o'clock. See that the Fleurus road is kept open. All the data that I have indicate that the Prussians cannot oppose us with more than 40,000 men.

These 'orders' read like a dictated monologue. The Emperor was thinking aloud, trying to clarify his decisions but without being completely successful.

In the letter to the Prince of Moscova the emphasis was placed on pushing on with all speed to Brussels, the occupation of which would cause the greatest reverberations. "Some clash with the English" was anticipated, but not a battle. Moreover, Ney had only some 40,000 to 50,000 men with which to oppose the enemy – if the Emperor did not withdraw the division under Marbais, the corps under Kellermann, or the light cavalry of the Guard. The mission entrusted to the Marshal was only of secondary importance and would become paramount only "in the evening or during the night" when the Emperor had "taken his decision to march on Brussels".

The order sent to Grouchy seemed to indicate that the Emperor himself wanted to complete the manoeuvre of Charleroi, begun the day before, with 40,000 or 50,000 men plus the Guard, if necessary, against the retreating Blücher's 'rearguards' – estimated at 40,000 men . . . The right flank would then screen the Emperor's march on the Belgian capital against all Prussian attacks. The state entry was already prepared . . .

Ligny. Battle on the bridge over the Ligne, near the farm of En Bas. By Knötel.

In the waggon train the Emperor's robes were ready, with the gold sword and the proclamations addressed to the Belgian people and to the inhabitants of the right bank of the Rhine: "Brussels. Imperial Palace of Laeken." They awaited only a date and a signature . . .

9.30 a.m. Napoleon was preparing to leave for Fleurus, which was occupied by Grouchy's cavalry, when an officer of the lancers arrived bearing a report from the left flank: the enemy was massed near Quatre-Bras. The Emperor ordered the 6th Corps – not mentioned in the letter to the marshals – to stay in front of Charleroi until further orders, and he had a communication sent to Marshal Ney to combine the corps under Reille, d'Erlon and Kellermann. With this force he had

"to fight and destroy all the enemy corps that might appear. Blücher was in Namur yesterday, and it is inconceivable that he has been able to bring up his troops to Quatre-Bras. So Ney will only have to deal with any coming from Brussels. Marshal Grouchy is going to Fleurus". It was there that reports had to be sent to the Emperor.

Napoleon considered, therefore, that troops arriving from Brussels would present little danger. His imagination seethed. He talked animatedly; the facts were taking shape in his mind just as he wanted them to be.

Underestimating the strength and bravery of his adversaries, he did not consider that Blücher and Wellington, 50 kilometres apart, would have the temerity to concentrate their resources

Battle of Ligny. At the lower right can be seen the columns of the grenadiers of the Guards, whose attack at the end of the day was to prove decisive. Lithograph by J. Grenier.

near the Imperial Army, which was drawn up in a solid block.

Until the morning of the 16th, it is true, neither the Prussian nor the British Commander-in-Chief had considered it either.

Blücher had been on horseback since daybreak – grumpy, bad-tempered and worried. From his headquarters at the Sombreffe rectory he had arrived at the Brye windmill, acclaimed by Ziethen's soldiers. From there he had anxiously surveyed the Fleurus plateau. If Napoleon attacked, he would have only the 1st Corps – not at full strength and exhausted – with which to oppose the French; his other troops would arrive only gradually. The 4th Corps was not due at Hannut (40 kilometres from Sombreffe) until that evening.

There was no news from Wellington. Major von Brünneck had gone to Quatre-Bras in search of von Müffling with a request for information about the Duke's intentions.

Wellington was still asleep, and his reserve troops were in disorder. Only General Picton, in civilian dress – shabby frock-coat, top hat, field-glass slung across his chest (his luggage had not arrived) – had left at 4 a.m. with the brigades under Kempt and Pack, drums beating, bagpipes wailing.

The Nassau battalions moved off at 9 a.m. As for the others . . . no one knew.

The gap from Charleroi to Brussels was to remain open for the best part of the day.

Wellington rose at 5 a.m., breakfasted with Dörnberg, mounted his horse at 8 a.m. and, followed by von Müffling – who was on the watch for any word or gesture from him – set off towards Genappe.

The Prince of Orange, wearing the full dress uniform of a British hussar, having left Brussels at 1.30 a.m., dismounted at 5 a.m. in the main square of Braine-le-Comte in front of the Hôtel du Miroir, his headquarters. The General Staff had worked well: the road to Brussels had been left open to the French, who had not taken advantage of it; Perponcher's division had been sent off towards Quatre-Bras; and Chassé's division had been alerted. Napoleon's cavalry was expected to appear from Frasnes at any moment.

On this night of alerts, no thought of co-ordination crossed the minds of the surprised leaders: no British manoeuvre was anticipated. No link-up between the Allied forces was planned. Gneisenau distrusted Wellington.

7 a.m. The Prince of Orange was at Quatre-Bras, where he received Major von Brünneck and gave him the British intelligence reports – which were incorrect: the Perponcher division would not, as he said, "meet up at Nivelles at 10 a.m.". By 9 a.m. the Prince had under his command at Quatre-Bras only 6,000 infantry and 8 guns.

If Ney had brought up his 20,000 men earlier, supported by the 50 guns . . . But he was awaiting – with what impatience – the Emperor's orders.

9.30 a.m. The Duke arrived at the crossroads and surveyed the horizon . . . Nothing . . . The Dutch were preparing soup . . . the French also . . . As usual, the danger had been exaggerated. Those gentlemen at Braine-le-Comte had taken ample precautions and had become alarmed too hastily. The action at Frasnes had been only a feint, probably designed to conceal a movement by Napoleon in the direction of Mons . . . In any event, Napoleon's present effort weighed only on the Prussians . . . Somewhat relieved by this reflection, the Duke decided at about 10 o'clock to write to Blücher . . .

At that moment the situation was as follows:

Wellington did not believe there would be a serious attack on Quatre-Bras by the French.

At Frasnes, Ney was impatiently waiting for orders to attack that did not come.

At Brye, Blücher was reading in a report from von Brünneck "Three enemy battalions are visible, two regiments of lancers . . . "; and he looked anxiously towards Frasnes, wondering what had happened to the French Army.

On the road to Charleroi, Napoleon imagined Blücher to be retreating towards the east and Wellington retreating towards the west.

10.15 a.m. Grouchy received La Bédoyère and learned that he was in command of the Emperor's right flank, the intention appearing to be to finish off the Prussians and then march on Brussels. After giving specific orders, he established at about 10.30 a.m. that the 3rd Corps (Vandamme) was approaching from Fleurus, followed by Milhaud's cuirassiers. The Guard, having left their bivouacs at 9 a.m., emerged from the woods in a cloud of dust.

The heat was stifling.

With his vanguard and right flank protected by Pajol and Exelmans, Grouchy decided to wait for the 4th Corps (Gérard) in order to attack the Prussians with all his resources.

11 a.m. Out in front, towards Ligny, gunfire could be heard and, behind this, ovations. It was the Emperor. According to the order of the day, there was to be no ceremony when His Majesty visited the advance posts.

What was happening out there?

The Emperor, up in the mill at Fleurus, discovers that the Prussian Army is massed at Brye.

The farm of En-Haut.

Nothing could be seen through the motionless fields of rye drooping in the heat, apart from a handful of Prussian troopers emerging from a fold in the terrain behind a mound called the 'Tomb of Ligny'.

The Emperor advanced across the plain as far as the Naveau windmill, near the tree-lined Sombreffe road. He ordered the sappers to build an observation post – a circular gallery around the windmill – and, map in hand, began to survey the scene to check the information supplied by the surveyor Simon (who subsequently received the Légion d'Honneur from Napoléon III).

The plain, gently undulating, was covered by growing crops but had deep cut-out escarpments to the east. To the north, the elm-planted road from Namur to Nivelles intersected the Charleroi-Sombreffe road at Le Point-du-Jour; a little to the south-west, the belfry and the Portriaux windmill; to the left, behind Wagnelée, the Roman road crossing the Nivelles road at the inn of Les Trois-Burettes. Straight ahead, about half a league away – a wood? No . . . it was the village of Saint-Amand, made up of isolated farms and houses surrounded by meadows and thickets. In the distance, in the direction of Ligny, the village belfry could just be discerned.

Saint-Amand was built on the right bank of the Ligne – a small winding river, about four to five metres wide, that slid through the plain between steep banks overgrown with

Major von Lützow, celebrated leader of the partisans in 1813. He was taken prisoner while attacking a square of the 4th Regiment of Grenadiers of the Guard at the head of the 6th Uhlans.

willows and bushes. On its way it passed through Ligny, from where the village belfry could equally well be seen among the greenery. There were two parallel roads running through the village – one on the right bank, the other on the left bank – connected by one stone bridge and a few wooden footbridges. To the west of Ligny there was a kind of fortress, the Château de Looz, that was dilapidated but still solid. Within the village there were farms that looked like fortresses; and the church, higher up on the right bank, was surrounded by a walled cemetery. Everywhere there were small alleys, cul-de-sacs and gardens – all of which lent themselves to defence.

Something arrested the Emperor's attention. Between the two villages and the ridge that dominated them it was possible with the aid of field-glasses to make out numbers of troops and, near a small wood and the Bussy windmill, a group of horsemen.

The Emperor could not see clearly what was happening towards Sombreffe. The Prussians seemed to be established on the line Saint-Amand-Ligny-Sombreffe – perpendicular to the Namur road, along which large elms formed a screen. Orientation was difficult because of the lack of relief, the angles formed by the roads, and the winding of the river.

Gradually, Napoleon realised that the Prussians were spread out before him in rapidly increasing numbers. Grouchy and Girard had been right. Units, if not columns, were emerging from Point-du-Jour. "The old fox won't want to break cover today," Napoleon commented.

Perhaps he was waiting for Wellington.

The two Allied commanders were, in fact, meeting at the Bussy windmill – within range of Napoleon's field-glass that had picked out a group of cavalry . . .

At 10.45 a.m., at Quatre-Bras, Wellington was re-reading the letter he had just written to Blücher:

On the heights of Frasnes
June 16, 1815, 10.30 a.m.

My dear Prince,
My army is situated as follows: the prince's corps has a division here and the rest at Nivelles. The reserve is on the way from Waterloo to Genappe, where it will arrive at noon. The English cavalry will be at the same time at Nivelles. Lord Hill's corps is at Braine-le-Comte.

The information was not correct. Wellington had been misled by his General Staff. Picton would arrive at Genappe at 3 p.m.; Hill's corps was en route for Enghien. Perponcher's division would not all be at Quatre-Bras until about 2 p.m.

Field-Marshal Blücher thrown down by a charge of the cuirassiers of the 9th Regiment. Count von Nostitz, his aide-de-camp, is beside him. Engraving by Philippoteaux.

A charge by uhlans saves Field-Marshal Blücher. His horse had been a present from the Prince Regent of England. Painting by Messerschmitt.

The Duke added:

I do not see many of the enemy in front of us. I await news from your Highness and the arrival of the troops in order to determine my operations for the day.

Nothing has been seen from the direction of Binche, nor on our right.

Just when he was about to hand over the letter to the "corpulent von Müffling" for transmission to the Field-Marshal, Wellington suddenly changed his mind.

Since Napoleon appeared to have selected the Prussians as his target, it would be interesting to find out Blücher's intentions . . . If he beat a retreat, for whatever reason, the Netherlands Army would be left to face the French on its own.

Followed by von Müffling, Dörnberg, Brunswick, Fitzroy Somerset and a few officers from the Royal Staff Corps, he spurred his horse towards Brye. The Duke was wearing a plain blue riding coat, a white cravat, a dark red belt, doe-skin breeches, and hussar-style boots with black tassels.

He was received between midday and 1 o'clock on the heights of Brye by Blücher, who was accompanied by Gneisenau, Grollmann and Hardinge.

From the top of the windmill their Excellencies observed on the Fleurus plain – the scene of many a combat between the east and the west – a sea of crops from which a few scattered villages emerged and, through field-glasses, the French columns moving up. The advance posts exchanged shots . . .

. . . and the generals exchanged remarks that have never been reported.

Were they having a battle of wits? It seems probable. English, German, Dutch, Belgian, Italian and French historians are still arguing about it. With due reservations, this is what is generally acknowledged to have taken place:

The ruins of burnt-out Ligny.

Wellington having asked what they expected of him, von Müffling suggested a concentration of the Anglo-Netherlands Army towards Frasnes and an attack on the French left flank; but Gneisenau suggested that the British Army should be directed along the Namur road, behind the Prussian Army, and held in reserve. Not wishing to be placed under Blücher's orders, the Duke suddenly became engrossed in studying his map . . . and, according to von Müffling, replied: "I shall come if I am not myself attacked." According to others, however, his reply was, "I shall overthrow what is in front of me and march on Gosselies." Be that as it may, after an exchange of views the two marshals separated without having planned mutual assistance in the event of attack but leaving Wellington with the conviction that, when it came to it, Blücher would do battle – which, for Wellington, was the main thing. As for Blücher, he came to the conclusion that it would be better to rely on himself rather than on the others; and he learned with relief that his 2nd Corps (von Pirch I) was approaching.

So the three army leaders, separated by only a league, each made an incorrect assessment of the situation.

Blücher did not know where 'Bonaparte' was; Wellington did not think that there would be a serious French attack on Quatre-Bras; Napoleon believed that he was confronted by only the Prussian rearguard and that the Anglo-Netherlands Army was to the west of the Charleroi-Brussels road.

Between 11 a.m. and 1 p.m. the veil was lifted.

The 2nd Prussian Corps reached Le Point-du-Jour. Its 1st Brigade went through Sombreffe and took up a position along the Nivelles road so that it would be in support of the 1st Corps, the brigades of which were drawn up thus: Pirch II on the heights of Brye; Jagow and Steinmetz at Saint-Amand; Henckel at Ligny.

On the road, the infantry of the 25th Prussian Regiment – wearing caps or shakos according to platoon – followed by the Westphalians in green, continued their march and stopped at Les Trois-Burettes, reconnoitring towards Quatre-Bras. They were followed by the rest of the 2nd Corps and then the 3rd Corps. The concentration of Blücher's troops, which had been prepared since May, was being carried out under the nose of the enemy. Provided that the French gave them a respite of three hours . . .

Fleurus, noon. Here was General Gérard, who later mentioned how eager he had been to get into the fighting. Why, then, did he not cross the Sambre earlier? His last two divisions did not arrive until 2 p.m. Having set off with a reconnais-

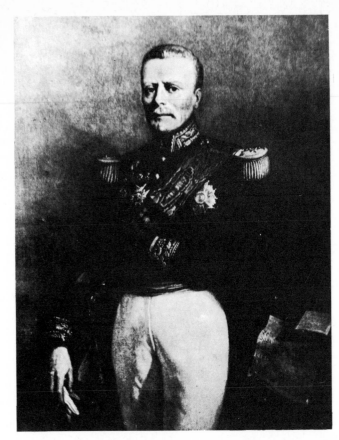

Lieutenant-General de Bonnemain, 1773–1850, commander of the 4th and 12th Dragoons, 2nd Cavalry Corps. After a portrait by Couture. Collection of Commandant Lachouque.

people from Brussels", would intervene on the right and rear of Blücher . . . "Not one cannon of his army will escape." Destruction completed, the French would then manoeuvre according to circumstances in order to slip away towards Brussels, bivouacking on the "mountain of savoury pot-herbs".

And Europe would bow before the glory of reconquest.

The Chief of Staff drafted the order for the Prince of the Moscova.

Straight ahead, the Prussian 2nd and 3rd Corps were closing on Sombreffe, Brye or Tongrinnes, bordering the river Ligne near the Potriaux windmill.

"If Ney carries out my orders correctly, it could be that in three hours the outcome of the war will have been decided," Napoleon soliloquised, dominated by his dream.

sance party in the direction of Sombreffe, he was immediately driven back by some of Lützow's volunteers; his Chief of Staff was pierced seven times by lances. As for himself, his horse tumbled into a ditch and he would have been killed but for the arrival of a squadron of the 12th Chasseurs led by Grouchy's son. Bruised, he was angered by this fall from his horse and by the desertion of Bourmont, for whom he was answerable . . . What would the Emperor say? Nothing, perhaps; or once again: "The Blues are always blue; the Whites, always white." More coarsely, Blücher, on seeing Bourmont pass later, refused to receive him, saying: "A cur is always a cur."

Hulot's division of the 4th Corps finally emerged from Fleurus. Napoleon was now completely ready for the battle that was brewing. Was he making allowances for his illusions? He was about to destroy the Prussian rear-guards in battle. Their right was not solidly supported . . . Therefore, a general attack: 3rd Corps on Saint-Amand; 4th Corps on Ligny; the Guard in reserve. Ney, who was confronted by only "the

The Gemioncourt farm.

French Infantry of the Line in 1815 (Field Dress).
1, grenadier; 2, drummer; 3, grenadiers officer; 4, drum-major; 5, field officer; 6, fusilier; 7, drummer.

Light Infantry in 1815.
1, bandsman; 2, voltigeurs in overcoats; 3, officer, voltigeurs; 4, fusilier; 5, cornet (bugle-hornist), voltigeurs.

94

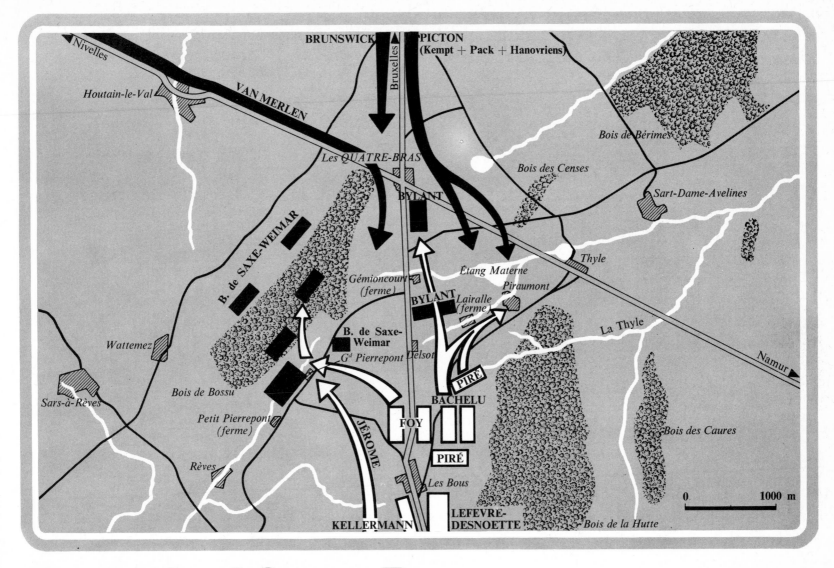

The battle of Quatre-Bras

Too tardily attacked by Marshal Ney's troops, launched in successive waves that they were lacking in support and co-ordination, Quatre-Bras – constantly consolidated by the arrival of fresh reinforcements (Van Merlen, Picton, Brunswick) – finally remained in Wellington's hands.

If the Prince of the Moscova had not lost the morning of the 16th by failing to make his infantry cross the few kilometres that separated it from the Prince of Orange's outposts, a sudden attack at midday by Reille's infantry would have been sufficient to dislodge from the crossroads the few defenders to be found there.

The crossroads at Quatre-Bras. Anonymous water-colour. Musée Royal de i'Armee, Brussels.

The battle of Quatre-Bras

Lieutenant-General Count Reille, 1775–1860, commander of the 2nd Corps. Collection of Commandant Lachouque.

At Quatre-Bras, Ney was fully engaged in battle.

He had left Frasnes in the early morning – not having seen from there anything more happening at Quatre-Bras than on the previous day – restless because he had received no orders from the Emperor and uneasy to learn from Girard of the "arrival of enemy concentrations coming down the road from Namur". The Prince of the Moscova had had an unpleasant morning. At his disposal was only Reille's corps and 34 guns. Two of d'Erlon's divisions had arrived at Jumet; the two others and the cuirassiers were at the rear.

The hours were pealed from the belfries. Certainly, if the Emperor had given the order to march earlier, Reille would easily have been able to crush the enemy posts since they were unable to see what was ahead of them. Probably... But beyond these posts what would they have found?

The Prince of Orange leading the Dutch-Belgians to the attack at the battle of Quatre-Bras. Engraving by Velyn, after a painting by Van Bree. Musée Royal de l'Armée, Brussels.

Bayonet-charge by the Scottish units of Picton's division on the Gemioncourt hillside. By Knötel.

Lieutenant-General Bachelu, commander of the 5th Infantry Division of the 2nd Corps. Musée de l'Armée, Paris.

General Foy, 1775–1825, commander of the 9th Infantry Division. He was seriously wounded during the Hougoumont attack on 18th June. Musée de l'Armée, Paris.

Marshal Ney, French commander at Quatre-Bras. After a drawing by Meissonnier. Private collection.

The Duke of Brunswick at the battle of Quatre-Bras. By J. Girbal, from Soldats et Uniformes du 1er Empire.

Death of the Duke of Brunswick.

Duke of Brunswick's infantry in action. By Knötel.

11 a.m. Flahaut arrived with the order dictated earlier at Charleroi by the Emperor. Ney read the document and then issued his own orders:

The 2nd Corps was to set off immediately. Bachelu's division would take up a position behind Genappe, covering the openings ahead on the Brussels road.

Foy's division would follow and take up positions to the right and left of Banterlez (1 kilometre north of Quatre-Bras).

Jérôme Napoléon's division, Girard's division and Reille's headquarters would be at Quatre-Bras.

The first three divisions of Count d'Erlon (1st Corps) would come to Frasnes; the right division would go to Marbais with the 2nd Corps cavalry (General Piré). Jacquinot's cavalry (1st Corps) would cover the march on Brussels.

The Marshal's headquarters and the cavalry under Lefebvre-Desnoëttes would be at Frasnes. The cuirassiers would be at Frasnes and Liberchies.

The order referred to the intention to march on Brussels that evening according to instructions given by the Emperor, who did not expect any resistance from that quarter.

Equally badly informed about the enemy, the Marshal wrote to Major-General Soult to report on the orders he had issued:

All the intelligence reports mention that there are about 3,000 infantry at Quatre-Bras but very little cavalry. It is my belief that the Emperor's plans for his march on Brussels will be carried out without serious obstacles.

The Prince of the Moscova has been accused of lack of initiative. Why did he not, early on 16th June, occupy the cross-roads at Quatre-Bras, which he knew to be defended by only a few battalions? He should have anticipated the Emperor's orders. But why did these not arrive until 11 o'clock? It was only four leagues from Charleroi to Frasnes.

Ney has also been criticised for his slowness in executing the orders.

The backroom strategists would do well to cool their ardour and consider the situation.

Ney must have read Napoleon's letter and re-read it, probably several times, since it was not easy to grasp . . . then he would have thought it over for a moment, made his marching preparations, dictated the order to Heymès (his only aide-de-camp) and sent it off to Reille.

The commander of the 2nd Corps would have done likewise and then drafted and despatched his own instructions to his generals, some of whom were ten kilometres away, and they in turn would have to set their regiments in motion.

The Duke of Brunswick, a few minutes after his death. Engraving by Vinkeles, after J. van Bree. Musée Royal de l'Armée, Brussels.

Monument to the memory of the Duke of Brunswick, erected on the spot where he was killed.

The British 28th Regiment of Foot at the battle of Quatre-Bras. Sketch by Captain Jones, from The Battle of Waterloo, *London, 1817.*

The 42nd Highlanders (the Black Watch), formed in square, under attack by General Piré's lancers. Black Watch Museum, Dalhousie Castle, Perth.

Major-General Sir Hussey Vivian, commander of the Anglo-German 6th Cavalry Brigade. His squadrons were engaged at the end of the battle and took part in the pursuit of the French Army.

The farm of Quatre-Bras.

The 28th Regiment of Foot – part of Kempt's brigade, in Picton's division – formed in square, resist the charges of the 1st and 6th Chasseurs à Cheval (Piré's division). In error, the artist has depicted the chasseurs in the uniform of the hussars.

Drouet d'Erlon was asked to make haste. Kellermann had to allow his cuirassiers to dismount since their horses were exhausted.

It is therefore hardly surprising that Marshal Ney's attack could not begin before 2 p.m. Even then, it was launched on the false data that fell apart at the seams before the divisions had as much as arrived at their positions. On both sides reinforcements were used with no idea of how to manoeuvre, and they were flung into the fire the moment they arrived. It was not so much a battle as a chance encounter on "a pocket handkerchief".

To the south of the crossroads, the roads from Charleroi to Brussels and from Nivelles to Namur – perhaps tree-lined – with very high banks, made a three-kilometre square situated between Frasnes, Villers-Perwin, Sart-Dame-Avelines and Houtain-le-Val. There were three small streams, a few dales and a ridge crested by the Bossu woods, which came down to the edge of the Namur road near the crossroads and ran for some 200 metres in an arc along the Charleroi road. The Gémioncourt farm was some 1,200 metres away from the Namur road. Further to the east was Pireaumont, with its marshy approaches, and the Lairalle farm – between which and Villers-Perwin were the La Hutte woods. At the crossroads there was a large farm, a few houses and the La Baraque tavern. Nothing special about the 'position'; a very restricted terrain; no emplacements for artillery. Such was the battle-field.

Covered by Piré's cavalry, supported by his artillery, Bachelu took Pireaumont and installed himself there. With one brigade Foy drove back the Dutch defending Gémioncourt, and he engaged the other in the Bossu woods. There was fierce fighting straight away. Perponcher's infantry, quickly engaged, suffered losses; and his artillery was dismounted. Wellington, returning from Brye, anxiously watched the Brussels road; and the Prince of Orange watched the Nivelles road. They were both looking for reinforcements.

3 p.m. Those reinforcements were immediately pitched into the battle: van Merlen's Dutch-Belgian cavalry against Piré's lancers and chasseurs, then Picton's Scottish troops and the Brunswick Corps; the rest followed.

During this time Jérôme Napoléon's division, which had arrived at last, was launched against Brunswick's infantry in the Bossu woods, flung into the fray without having time to recover its breath. There was a fierce struggle. At the cross-roads the 92nd Highlanders, formed in square, shot point-blank some light dragoons . . . Belgians wearing the uniforms of French chasseurs.

4 p.m. Convinced that there would be little resistance, Ney had thrown all his available forces into the battle in an attempt to gain the objectives set by the Emperor. The rapid but disjointed attacks of the 2nd Corps had not been able to reach these targets. And the enemy was being reinforced minute by minute.

Additionally, an order sent by the Emperor at 2 o'clock from Fleurus had disturbed Ney: "Grouchy is attacking an enemy corps established between Sombreffe and Brye," wrote Soult. "His Majesty's intention is that you should attack the forces in front of you and, having thrust against them vigorously, fall back upon us to assist in surrounding this corps."

Thrust against the enemy vigorously! But the Prince of the Moscova had been doing nothing but that since 2 p.m. The Emperor had kept Girard's division in front of Saint-Amand without him, Ney, having been definitely forewarned. D'Erlon's 1st Division would not reach the Roman road until about 4.30 p.m.

Bare-headed, sword in hand, Ney commanded the divisions of the 2nd Corps to attack once more in strength. They would be supported by 42 guns.

Before Ligny, 3 p.m. Torrid heat. Being present, the Emperor assumed command. Grouchy had rejoined his cavalry on the right.

Colonel Baron Galbois, 1778–1850, commander of the 6th Regiment of Chevau-Légers-Lanciers (Piré's division). Painting by Pingret. Private collection.

King's colour of the 2nd Battalion of the 69th Regiment of Foot (the South Lincolnshires).

Death of Colonel Macara, commander of the 42nd Highlanders. Sketch by Captain Jones, from The Battle of Waterloo, *London, 1817.*

Lieutenant-General Sir Edward Barnes, 1776–1838. By George Dawe. Apsley House.

Colonel John Cameron, commanding officer of the 92nd Highlanders. After a portrait by C. Turner.

Near Saint-Amand, around the chapel of the Bon-Dieu-de-Pitié, the battalions of Lefol's division (3rd Corps), which had been lying concealed in the crops, arose. The veterans knocked out their pipes against the butt-ends of their muskets; the conscripts, necks stretched, straightened their backs under the weight of their packs. Square-formed, the division listened to Lefol on horseback: "The battle is about to begin . . . the Prussians will be crushed as they were at Jena . . . Victory . . ."

Near the windmill, the cannon of the Guard fired three times. A great shout went up: "Long live the Emperor!"

With the 15th Light at their head, Lefol led the 23rd, 37th and 64th on to Saint-Amand. The drums beat the charge. The band of the 23rd, entangled in the growing crops, played "Le Chant du Départ, la Victoire en chantant" sweeping into

Sir Edward Barnes mustering his faithful 92nd Highlanders. At 6 p.m., when the situation became critical, they launched a desperate counter-attack. Water-colour by J. Girbal, from Soldats et Uniformes du 1er Empire.

102

Saint-Amand behind the 'greens' of the 7th Prussian Regiment. But they were unable to cleave their way through the enemy, being overthrown by the Brandenburgers under Steinmetz. The cannon roared; each house became a citadel; there was hand-to-hand fighting.

In the second line, a surge of shakos with copper eagles swerved to the left. Vandamme was pushing Berthezène beyond Saint-Amand.

General Girard threw the 11th Light (ex-sharp-shooters from Corsica and the Po Valley) against Le Hameau and La Haye. His division, drawn up facing the east, took the village. "Courage, lads! Lead to the right! Close the ranks! Charge!" They reached the Brye crest. The artillery was striking the rear of the 'greens' defending Ligny . . . Blücher's right wing was surrounded . . .

From his position near the Bussy windmill, old 'Vorwärts' saw the danger too late and flung an infantry brigade to the front and two cavalry regiments to the flank. Terror reigned in La Haye . . . Pursuits through the streets were followed by the bloody conflicts of the 4th of the Line, the 12th Light and the 6th Prussian Regiment. Girard forced back the Westphalians before him and then fell, mortally wounded.

"Young men! Keep yourselves worthy! Forward, in God's name!" Blücher shouted to the soldiers under Pirch II, who were pushing before them the survivors of Girard's division mustered by Colonel Matis. Twenty officers of the 11th Light, almost all Corsican, were out of the fight: Parmegiani, the battalion commander; Captain Mattei and Captain Casalto; Lieutenant Bonnifacci and standard-bearer Bastiani among others. The 12th Light lost 25; the 4th of the Line lost 25; the 86th lost 10 . . . and at Wagnelée the 2nd and 25th Prussian Regiments of the Line were decimated by Habert's division.

Eighteen battalions of the 4th Corps deployed in front of Ligny and facing north-west – that is, almost at right-angles to the 3rd Corps – departed at the same time, their bands in the lead, to attack the village. There were cries of "Long live the Emperor!"

Henckel's skirmishers, who had been entrenched in the houses and the farm at En-Bas, in the Château of Looz and in the cemetery of En-Haut, came out and took cover behind fences, walls and hedges. They were soon reinforced by the 19th Prussian Regiment and the 4th Westphalian Landwehr, receiving the assailants with a hail of shot from 24 guns.

These guns were quickly silenced by Gérard's artillery supported by batteries of the Guard, which tore apart the village defences. Ligny was ablaze from end to end. Through

Lieutenant-General Kellermann, Count of Valmy, 1770–1835, commander of the 3rd Cavalry Corps. Collection of Commandant Lachouque.

At the end of the day, General Kellermann – who led the charge of Guiton's brigade (8th and 11th Cuirassiers) – had his horse killed beneath him. He regained the French positions by hanging on to the stirrups of two troopers. Drawing by V. Huen. Collection of Commandant Lachouque.

At the end of the battle of Quatre-Bras, Wellington gives the order to attack to Kempt's brigade. Sketch by Captain Jones, from The Battle of Waterloo, *London, 1817.*

R. Desvarreux.
1903.

Major-General Van Merlen, commander of the 2nd Light Cavalry Brigade of the Dutch-Belgian cavalry. Former Colonel-Major of the lancers of the Imperial Guard, he was killed at Waterloo.

a hell of fire and shot, the 30th Regiment of the Line penetrated the En-Haut road to the beat of the drums. They were followed by the brigades of Schoeffer and Le Capitaine. Amid the flames and smoke, the flashes of cannons, the crashing of tumbling walls, the screams of the wounded who were being burned alive, the devils of Henckel and Jagow hurled out their hatred. The 30th Regiment lost all of its senior officers; the 63rd lost its colonel; General Le Capitaine was killed.

The blue-clad mob maintained a relentless pursuit of the 'green' rabble right up to the cemetery, among the crosses on the graves and between bloodstained tombstones. Bayonets broke against the church flagstones, one of them pinning a sergeant to the church door. Outside, a shako fell with its owner's head still in it. Teeth caked with powder, tongues blackened, musket-muzzles scorched, cartridge-pouches empty, the attackers continued with musket-butts and stones on both sides of the river Ligne – congested with the dead – until the combatants fell exhausted with only

Ligny. General von Gneisenau directs the retreat on Wavre during the night of 16th to 17th June. By Knötel.

enough strength to shake a fist or snap their fingers at their opponents...

They had forgotten the other Fleurus – Jena – these 'rough greens'. They had thought that the Saxon affrays of Leipzig and the treacheries of Fontainebleau would start up again... and now it was happening.

Their shakos holed, their moustaches burnt, these devils finally broke down, breathless.

With the dead piled up and the wounded clustered together in the ruins of the crushed village, it was not always easy to distinguish between them.

Blücher had been persistent, Gérard had been stubborn – and Ligny was not taken.

To the right, facing the windmill of Potriaux, Hulot's division was at grips with von Borcke's and Kemphen's brigades of the 3rd Prussian Corps. From Sombreffe to Fleurus the battle raged; the cavalries charged each other – the uhlans of Marwitz, the dragoons of Exelmans, the hussars of von Lottum. Some horses fell; others, riderless, galloped around in the smoke and finally tumbled into the river Ligne. Squares were formed against these fantastic overlapping charges. And the fighting went on and on in this square kilometre of fire. There were 24,000 French stubbornly battling against 28,000 Prussians.

Towards 5 o'clock, Blücher called up his reserves and tried to get through on his right. All of his artillery was blazing away. Facing him, Vandamme occupied Wagnelée, Le Hameau and Saint-Amand, and he too had just brought up his last reserves – the Swiss battalion under Colonel Stoffel. The forces in the field seemed to balance each other. While Napoleon was sending Colbert's lancers to the left, Blücher was directing Marwitz's uhlans to his right.

It was necessary that Ney, having repulsed the "lot from Brussels", should be able to contain them with Reille and send d'Erlon and half the cuirassiers to attack Marbais.

At the Fleurus windmill, under heavy storm-clouds, his forehead beaded with perspiration to which a lock of hair was sticking, hands crossed over the tails of his green coatee, fingers clenching feverishly, Napoleon strode up and down on the flour-coated floorboards and kept vigil...

On a map nailed to a beam, the name 'Marbais' had been underlined ten times.

"If d'Erlon carries out the order that you have stipulated to Ney," Soult said, "the Prussian Army is lost."

Napoleon did not reply, watching the mustering of his reserves. The 6th Corps had been recalled from Charleroi at about 3.30. Behind Vandamme there were eight battalions of the Young Guard led by Duhesme, who had already distinguished himself here on 25th June 1794. Further away, behind Michel – who had been in the Guard since 1805 – there were three regiments of chasseurs à pied of the Middle and Old Guard under the command of Henrion (4th Corps), Malet (3rd Corps) and Pelet (2nd Corps).

Behind the 4th Corps were the sole battalion of the 4th Grenadiers (Harlet) and the 3rd (Poret de Morvan).

To the west, the cannons from Quatre-Bras thundered loudly. Napoleon knew from Janin, Chief of Staff of the 6th Corps, that Ney was very heavily engaged. Sent to Frasnes by Count de Lobau for news, Janin had seen the Marshal there at about 4.15, finding him at grips with 20,000 English, Scottish and Dutch. Ney had at his disposal only four divisions from the cavalry of the 2nd Corps and from a brigade of cuirassiers. He had been counting on the assistance of the 1st Corps to overcome the British resistance and march on Marbais in accordance with the Emperor's order, and he had no information about Count d'Erlon. A little earlier, the General had arrived seeking news and had been in Frasnes conversing with the cavalry generals of the Guard; but since then he had disappeared. Furious, the Prince of the Moscova had instructed Janin to inform the Emperor of his situation: he was without resources and had no Chief of Staff. Then he had moved off at a gallop to rejoin an attacking column.

At Quatre-Bras Bachelu had, in fact, gone back to the offensive against Pireaumont and the furthermost parts of Gémioncourt but had been halted by the fire from Pack's Scots and Kempt's battalions, which had been driven back from another position by the 108th of the Line and Piré's lancers.

To the left, cannonballs and shells were mowing down the files of Brunswickers who had been holding out desperately near the crossroads. These sombre infantrymen wavered before Bauduin's skirmishers, sent by Prince Jérôme into the open space between the road and the Bossu woods. The Duke of Brunswick, looking wan, dressed in black, a béret on his head, lit a pipe, snapped his fingers at death – whose grinning emblem he had given to his hussars – and launched his cavalry on Bauduin's infantry. His troops were quickly decimated, the survivors, with Piré in hot pursuit, spreading panic as far as the crossroads. The Duke did his best to check his scattered battalions, but Death had singled him out and he fell at the place where to this day stands the monument erected to his memory.

And Wellington himself escaped Piré's death-dealers only by the grace of the mighty muscles of his thoroughbred horse Copenhagen.

Ney had not left the front line.

5 o'clock. La Bédoyère, aide-de-camp to the Emperor, presented himself to Ney: he had brought a pencilled note, unsigned, in which His Majesty ordered the 1st Corps to fall back on Blücher's right to achieve the destruction of the Prussians. The general added that the order was in the course of being carried out: he had encountered the head of the column on his way and had diverted it to the direction in which it should go; Count d'Erlon had been informed.

It seems, however, that the Emperor, Soult and the French General Staff knew nothing about this note.

Between 5 o'clock and 5.30, Gérard took the church and the château of Ligny. A battery of cannons in the cemetery pulverised three battalions under von Jagow. Two brigades of the 3rd Corps advanced, drums beating. They struck with axes in the de la Tour farm. In the street of En-Haut and those

of En-Bas, the slain were thrown into the flames. The shells from the Guard rained down on the thatched roofs, which immediately caught fire.

To the left, the front cracked under the weight of Tippelskirch and von Krafft of the 2nd Corps. The soldiers under Matis evacuated Le Hameau; Berthèzene's troops withdrew; Lefol's exhausted regiments panicked before Pirch's devils – fresh battalions with white and black guidons. The smoke was so dense that it was impossible to distinguish blue from green, and men struck blindly at each other.

On the French right flank, the Prussian 3rd Corps was immobilised by Grouchy's troops. For a long time action was confined to an artillery duel and feints by cavalry.

In touch with Ligny through the squadrons of the 1st Corps, Thielmann's brigades occupied the heights of Sombreffe, Point-du-Jour and Tongrinne – a front of three kilometres with outposts at the Potriaux windmill, Tongrinelle, Boignée and Balatre.

Towards 4 p.m., Hulot's skirmishers attacked Tongrinelle

General map of operations on the day after Ligny

On the 17th, Napoleon rejoined Ney at Quatre-Bras and drove the English back to their defensive position at Mont-Saint-Jean. Meanwhile, the Prussians – pursued by 30,000 French troops led too slowly and too far afield by Grouchy – took up a position at Wavre on the left bank of the Dyle river. On the 18th – while Thielmann faced Grouchy on that river – Ziethen, Bülow and Pirch made a breakthrough on Napoleon's right flank, which was then engaged in combat with Wellington. This intervention decided the Allied victory.

With this map it is possible to follow the retreat of Grouchy's corps on the 19th and 20th June from Rosières and La Bawette up to Namur, passing through Gembloux, at the cost of combats at La Falise and Le Boquet.

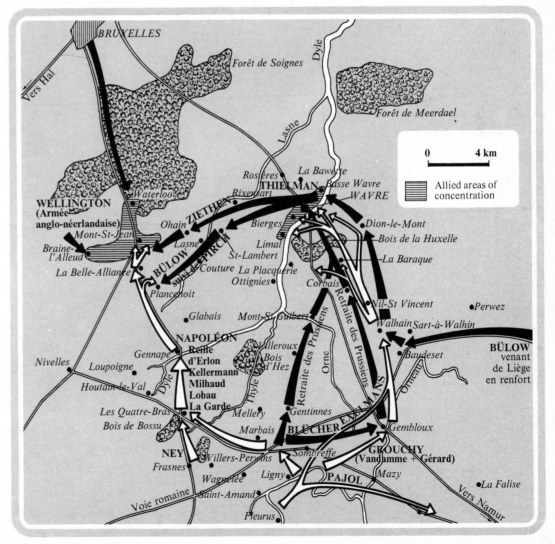

Lieutenant-Colonel von Sohr, commander of a brigade of the cavalry reserve of the Prussian 2nd Corps.

Fleurus. Château de la Paix as it is today. Napoleon slept there on the night of 16th to 17th June.

and were driven back by Kemphen's brigade; but an hour later the Prussians were chased off by Pajol's troopers supported by two battalions.

Towards 6.30 p.m. Prussian units deployed between Potriaux, Sombreffe and Tongrinelle lined the Ligne river with their skirmishers. A double line of infantry and artillery spread over 8,000 metres, from Wagnelée to Tongrinelle.

Napoleon decided to be done with it. Since he could no longer count on Ney, he mounted his manoeuvre in front of Ligny. The reserves of the Guard, led by Gourgaud, were on their way when Vandamme signalled that one league to his left a column of unknown nationality was emerging from the wood at La Hutte.

Awaiting the return of reconnaissance parties, the Emperor prudently decided to halt the advance of the reserves but gave the order to attack to the Guard, drawn up behind the 3rd and 4th Corps. Cheered by Vandamme's exhausted soldiers, the Young Guard – under Duhesme and Barrois – stormed the ruins of Le Hameau, cluttered with trampled corpses, and pressed on beyond the willows bordering the stream held by the 2nd and 4th chasseurs à pied and those of the 3rd Corps who were still able to walk. The cavalry under Domon and Colbert overthrew the squadrons of von Sohr and von Thümen, who was mortally wounded.

The 3rd Chasseurs à Pied, who had been sent to the left to observe the mysterious column, now knew what it was. So did the officer sent by the Emperor . . . It was Count d'Erlon's 1st Corps. An hour before, the head of the column had been three-quarters of a league away from Saint-Amand.

Praise be to God! But why had Ney sent it in this direction? Surprised but reassured, the Emperor directed no order to d'Erlon but alerted his reserves waiting in position before Ligny.

In Quatre-Bras, the mystery deepened. La Bédoyère had just left Marshal Ney when one of the Chief of Staff's officers handed the marshal a note.

In front of Fleurus. 3.30.
I wrote to you an hour ago that the Emperor would attack the enemy at 2.30 in the position taken between the villages of Saint-Amand and Brye. At the moment, the action is very pronounced. His Majesty has instructed me to inform you that you must manoeuvre edgewise so as to encircle the enemy's right flank, and give them a good pummelling in their rear: this army is lost if you act vigorously; the fate of France is in your hands.

But what to obey? Good God! Had everyone, including the Emperor, lost his head? "The fate of France is in your hands" – and they were taking from him the means of operating.

Beside himself with fury, in the midst of whining musket-balls, covered with earth from shot that he wished "would hit him in the belly", Ney, raving, read and re-read papers, orders and notes.

But . . . on reflection, that pencilled note . . . not signed by Soult or the Emperor.

Delcambre, Chief of Staff to the 1st Corps, came on behalf of his commander to inform the marshal that his troops were marching on Saint-Amand by order of the Emperor, arriving in the middle of the Prince of the Moscova's seething cogitations and therefore receiving a good dressing down.

Motionless, hat off, the general listened to remarks that he did not understand . . . The pencilled note was not signed . . . ? The Chief of Staff had written that very morning to say "there will not be any difficulty about your orders being obeyed when you are detached" . . . ? All of this was accompanied by a stream of oaths, followed by a peremptory order to bring back the 1st Corps to Frasnes without delay.

After which, having relieved his bad temper, Ney mounted his third horse to attempt a supreme offensive and called Kellermann, who did not know exactly where his cuirassiers were . . . He had no news of Roussel's division . . . Picquet's brigade, of l'Héritier's division, was still far away; but the 8th and 11th (Guiton's brigade) were in front of Frasnes.

The 1st Light, and the 1st, 2nd and 3rd of the Line of Jérôme's division were approaching the crossroads; those of Bachelu and Foy climbed up into the rye to the right of the road, ready to jump on to the Namur highway. Kielmansegge's Hanoverians and Colin Halkett's British troops, coming from Nivelles, were caught under the French artillery fire and decimated. The 92nd Gordon Highlanders, launched against Bachelu, left their colonel and 25 officers and 260 men dead on the field.

Kellermann shook hands with the marshal and moved off at the head of 700 of Guiton's cuirassiers – Guiton having led the squadrons of the 1st Regiment of this arm at Eylau. Supported by the artillery, they advanced – but the smoke was so thick that they could see nothing . . .

But yes! A red square in distress. It had been cut down with swords and dislocated by the 8th, who had gone off with a colour. It was that of the 69th. The 11th Cuirassiers surrounded a square of the 30th British Foot but were overthrown at the crossroads. Kellermann, unhorsed, returned to the lines with a sprained ankle, hatless, clinging to the bridles of two horses. The survivors of this cavalcade clambered down the slope between the wood and the road, thrusting aside the infantry of Jérôme and Foy and not stopping until they reached the ambulances in Frasnes.

Ney, whose fifth horse had just fallen, flung himself among Foy's skirmishers. It had to be finished. Finished here . . . with all those who loomed up from the hollows and appeared on the main roads and the plain: British, Dutch, the Guards, who were now coming into the line . . . seven new batteries.

Seven o'clock tolled from the Frasnes belfry . . .

. . . And also from the Fleurus belfry. Stifling heat. Heavy black clouds rolling across the sky.

The Emperor was at the head of the Guards and his reserves. Not being able to surround Blücher, he was going to attack him in the centre.

The infantry of the Guard were marching in battalion columns at half-distance. Count Friant, an ex-sergeant of the Gardes Français (the heroes of Auerstädt and Moscow), and Comte Morand – like Friant a veteran of the Egyptian campaign, and his comrade in the glory of the 3rd Corps – were marching at their head. 'Père Roguet' was on horseback in front of Christiani's 2nd Grenadiers, which followed General Petit, at the head of the 1st, who the previous year had been embraced in the courtyard of Fontainebleau by the Emperor.

About two hundred metres to the left were the 1st Chasseurs à Pied under the command of Cambronne, who was famous for several brilliant actions.

Behind, Boissonnet's pioneer-sappers were with the marines of the couragous Tailhade.

In a great clanking of vehicles and steel, the artillery reserve advanced on the right flank with eight guns abreast, preceded by General Desvaux de Saint-Maurice and General Lallemand, and then 800 grenadiers à cheval, 800 of Baron Guyot's dragoons and 1,600 cuirassiers under Delort – that magnificent cavalry commander.

The approach march lasted twenty minutes under the rumbling of a thunderstorm.

And then, amid the thunder of God and man, the avalanche of 20,000 men overflowed into the smoking ruins of Ligny and what remained of the 21 battalions of von Henckel, von Jagow, von Krafft and Langen ordered by Blücher to hold out at all costs. The village was taken to the refrain of the "Chant du Départ".

8.45 p.m. The sun had set, but there was still the red of fires to be seen under the dark clouds in the direction of the La Hutte woods. To the north of the Brye ridge, uhlans, dragoons, and men of the Kurmak Landwehr were galloping in disorder to shouts of "Marsch! Marsch!", which had been the order to charge since the time of Frederick the Great. The 6th Black Uhlans under Lützow were decimated by the 4th Grenadiers. The Prince, 13 officers, and 70 troopers swept down to within 20 metres of the square.

Further away, in front of the Le Loup woods, old Blücher ran up, cloak streaming in the wind, to stop the débâcle. "In the Devil's name, attack, then!" he shouted to Roeder's troopers before falling in the midst of the 9th Cuirassiers. "I am lost!" he cried out to Count Nostitz as he fell. Hoisted on to a horse, he was evacuated without having been recognised by the French. A few squadrons of the Queen's Dragoons and of Brandenburg, led by Treskow, flung themselves courageously into the fray, thereby saving some of the army and also the honour of the Prussian cavalry – so much abused by contemporaries. What a "terrifying spectacle" it was, this "Todenritt" in the shadows of the flickering flames. Hobe's squadrons eventually gave way to the swords of Delort and the dragoons of the Guard that slowly followed the squares of Michel and Christiani.

Gneisenau had taken over the command. Around Ligny, the confusion was total. At the Brye windmill Langen, endeavouring to withdraw his brigade in good order, was mortally wounded. Krafft, who had lost 1,500 men, mustered a small group of soldiers on the road to Namur; Jagow still occupied Brye; a few of von Henckel's units withdrew towards Sombreffe.

To the right, the dragoons, uhlans, and hussars of Major General von Wahlen-Jurgäss – who had been ordered to cover the retreat – withdrew before Durette's and Jacquinot's divisions, which had been left on watch by d'Erlon before he, in accordance with Ney's orders, went to Frasnes; von Brause reached the Namur road; Tippelskirch reached Marbais; von Sohr's hussars and three battalions held out at Brye. Finally, the general retreat to Tilly took place along the forest paths while Ziethen mustered the few survivors of the cavalry in case of pursuit by the enemy.

On the Prussian left, Vichery's division of the 4th French Corps overthrew the squares of Steinmetz and Henckel near Sombreffe; Hulot's division, having seized the Potriaux windmill, had opened the way for the cavalry of the 4th Corps (General Maurin). Two regiments of Exelmans' dragoons overthrew Lottum's brigade. Four battalions under Borcke and Stülpnagel organised the resistance at Sombreffe after a fashion.

At about 9.30 p.m., the 6th Corps passed through Ligny and took up its position on the plateau of the Brye windmill in a sultry atmosphere, against a nightmarish background and within range of the Prussian outposts, which remained there throughout the night.

On the plain, the band of the French 1st Grenadiers played "La Victoire est à nous", and this tune was picked up and repeated by what remained of the regimental bands and trumpeters.

It certainly was a victory: with 65,000 men – of whom he had lost 12,000 – Napoleon had worn down 87,000 Prussians, whose numbers had that evening been reduced by at least 20,000. It was now necessary to finish it off.

Ten kilometres away to the north-west, an equally savage struggle had drawn to an end.

Wellington had joined battle with 35,000 men, of whom 5,000 had been killed or wounded. Uxbridge's cavalry had arrived at nightfall, tired out. But having returned that evening to sleep at the Hotel du Roi d'Espagne at Genappe, the Duke did not yet know the outcome of the Ligny battle.

Blücher was hoping for some aid from the English, but Gneisenau expected none.

In the clear night, the magnificent divisions of the Prince of the Moscova dressed their wounds. A fifth of his 20,000 men were out of the fight. The houses in Frasnes and Gosselies were full of wounded; and the farm at Quatre-Bras was a hell – for if the French medical service was precarious, the British had none at all. A surgeon made three attempts to amputate the leg of Colonel Hamilton of the 30th British, then he gave up . . . and the colonel kept his leg.

In conformity with Wellington's orders, the troops bivouacked where they were when the fighting stopped. The 1st and 2nd Brigades of Foot Guards established themselves to the north of the crossroads: the Nassau and Brunswick troops were around the Bossu woods.

In the wood, Jérôme's infantry withdrew metre after metre. Five hundred men and 130 British officers had remained in the scrub. When night fell, the division stopped at the Pierrepont farms: Foy's forces in front of Gémioncourt and Bachelu's infantry facing Pireaumont. The men fell exhausted beside their dead and wounded comrades. The gunners slept on their gun-carriages while someone went to look for full ammunition waggons . . .

Count d'Erlon, joined by Delcambre, had returned to Frasnes and taken over the advance posts from Reille.

It wanted but one hour and a march of three kilometres to destroy Blücher and turn Waterloo into a victory.

What had happened? What was the meaning of 17,000

The eve of Waterloo. Under torrential rain, Napoleon – at the head of the duty squadrons – directs the pursuit of the English rearguard, which is fleeing in great disorder. (Captain Mercer was to call it a "fox-hunt" in his memoirs.) Painting by Henri Charretier. Musée de l'Armée, Paris.

infantry, 17,000 cavalry and 6 guns marching into the midst of 500 thundering cannons, and of 200,000 men fighting desperately in a savage struggle? Neither the Emperor nor Soult could have summoned them to Saint-Amand since they had been surprised, nay, uneasy to see them arrive. Moreover, having been informed by Janin of Ney's situation, Napoleon would not have taken half his infantry away from the marshal. The order had not emanated from the Prince of the Moscova. Count d'Erlon had not, in the meantime, taken the initiative to move the troops. His following letter confirms what is already known:

Towards 11 a.m. or midday, Marshal Ney sent me an order to place my army corps under arms and direct it towards Frasnes and Quatre-Bras, where I would receive further orders.

This, in fact, concerned the order given by Ney after having received from Flahaut, at about 11 a.m., the Emperor's first letter. Continuing, d'Erlon wrote:

My army corps therefore began to move immediately, and after ordering the general in command of the head of the column [this was Durutte] to make the greatest possible speed I went on ahead to find out what was happening at Quatre-Bras, where it seemed to me that General Reille's corps was fighting. Beyond Frasnes, I stopped with the generals of the Guard, where I was reunited with General La Bédoyère, who showed me a pencilled note that he was taking to Marshal Ney and which charged the marshal to direct my army corps on Ligny. General La Bédoyère informed me that he had already given the order for this movement by changing the direction of my column, and he showed me where I could rejoin it. I immediately took this route and sent my Chief of Staff, General Delcambre, to Marshal Ney to inform him of my new destination.

Did General La Bédoyère have the authority to change the direction of my column before having seen the marshal? I do not think so . . .

So an order – a pencilled note – had been seen by both the marshal and Count d'Erlon. It is true that it was not signed and was not entered in the Chief of Staff's order book; but it was carried by General La Bédoyère, the Emperor's aide-de-camp. Had the impetuous general taken it upon himself to draft the order and have it executed when he heard, shortly after the battle began, a forceful and impatient wish that Ney would soon be able to intervene against the Prussian right?

La Bédoyère was shot on 19th August 1815. And not the Emperor at Saint Helena, or Soult, who died in 1851, or any of their contemporaries ever made any allusion to the event ... Opaque darkness ...

All of these military men knew that in war one does not do as one pleases and that a battle is a test in which the most solid bodies can dissolve, the clearest minds might become clouded and the most laudable initiatives could provoke catastrophes.

But later on the critics expressed surprise, shock; sometimes mockingly, sometimes indignantly. They tried to find the causes and, above all, those responsible for this regrettable incident, summoning before their tribunals the spirits of the performers and the long-vanished witnesses. Count d'Erlon was not accused of treason – but he had a narrow escape. In France avenging posterity has had no need of a traitor for 16th June, it is true, since Ligny ended up as a French victory.

It was a tactical victory, achieved following a desperate struggle pursued to the ruin of the Prussians' balance due to an accumulation of troops on their right and a premature wastage of their reserves. Blücher had more men than Napoleon but no other means at his disposal, whereas the Emperor had strength in reserve.

From the strategic point of view, victory could have been complete if instant advantage had been taken of the position. The 6th Corps was intact; the Guard, the cavalry reserve, and the cavalry divisions attached to the army corps had suffered little. The success should have been immediately exploited by an implacable pursuit until the Prussian Army had been destroyed. The campaign could have been half won that night.

Napoleon's attack at the centre had resulted in the retreat of the flanks; but they were able to withdraw in an order relative to their artillery. The defence of Brye and Sombreffe was being organised while Ziethen and Pirch – their forces seriously reduced – were disappearing into the woods towards Tilly and Mellery.

Rapid orders were required ... But minutes passed ... Then hours ...

The 3rd Corps, the Young Guard and some of the Old Guard set up wretched bivouacs outside La-Haye. The 4th Corps camped to the north of Ligny. The cuirassiers, under Delort, were to the east. Hulot, Pajol and Exelmans were in front of Sombreffe and at Tongrinne. The rest of the Old Guard was at Fleurus.

The Prussians were free – in disorder, but safe.

The forward posts of Jagow were established at Brye; those of Krafft were deployed the length of the road; those of Henckel, Stülpnagel and Borcke were installed at Sombreffe: all within range of the muskets of the French outpost guards. The grenadiers of the Guards bivouacked without fires, in battalions drawn up in squares and with one rank under arms. Hulot's sentries could hear sounds from the Prussians. Shouts of "To arms!", followed by rolling fire, gave rise to some alarm: the 75th of the Line fired on the 11th.

The Emperor returned to the château of Fleurus and retired to his bed, ill. He did not receive Grouchy, who had come to ask for his orders. Afterwards, summoning him a little too late, Napoleon told Grouchy to follow the enemy with the light cavalry.

Napoleon thought the Prussians had been crushed, with a loss of 30,000 men on the battlefield and 20,000 'dispersed'. Each to his own addition . . . Blücher therefore still had 30,000 beaten men plus Bülow's corps – 45,000 men in all. Napoleon no longer regarded these defeated troops as a danger: disorganised, cut up, they would need several days to recover. They could muster again only in some sheltered place, far from the victorious forces – maybe towards Namur in the east or Louvain in the north.

Tomorrow he would carry out the march on Brussels, as planned. The business at Quatre-Bras – during which Ney, with only 20,000 combatants, had resisted a large part of the Army of the Low Countries – proved that Wellington would not be able to stand up to him.

5. 17th June 1815

The pursuit of Blücher and Wellington

Le Point-du-Jour – the old Gembloux road used by the 3rd Corps on the night of 16th to 17th June and by Grouchy's corps on the afternoon of the 17th.

Genappe. The Hôtel du Roi d'Espagne in which Wellington slept on 16th June, Jérôme Bonaparte on the 17th and Blücher on the 18th.

By dawn the Prussian Army had evacuated the battlefield. Units of the 1st and 2nd Corps, badly battered, reached Tillery, Mellery and Gentinnes. Those of the 3rd Corps and the convoys reached Gembloux. The 4th halted at Beaudecet on learning of the defeat.

At the bivouacs between Tongrinne and Balâtre – where the feed for the horses was more damp heather and trampled rye-grass than fodder and the men ate what they could 'find' in the villages – the vedettes of the squadrons on outpost guard duty signalled at about 2 o'clock that the uhlans were evacuating Onoz. Grouchy gave the order to mount and ransack Sombreffe; Pajol, whose corps had been reduced to two regiments, gathered up the drunkards and the stragglers on the Namur road; the 5th Hussars put the disordered uhlans to the sword and captured eight pieces of artillery . . .

Pajol was following a false trail, and his engagement was without benefit. The captured battery had been roaming since dusk in search of the artillery of the park. The uhlans and the Prussian infantry had escaped, but Pajol could not know this and continued to look for them on the Namur road. Grouchy sent Exelmans, who had struck camp at about 4 a.m., to help him. Berton's brigade (the 14th and 17th Dragoons) followed the hussars; but like them, soon realising that the road was empty, Berton veered to the north. He shortly learned that the Prussians were at Gembloux, took note of it and . . . watched.

Grouchy arrived at the Château de la Paix. The previous evening he had received no order to pursue the enemy, so the Emperor was not surprised to find him at the 'Palace'. Besides, what was the use of going in pursuit if it meant riding the horses to death in the process? The Prussians were fleeing in disorder. Pajol's information only confirmed what Napoleon had been thinking. At about 8 a.m., during his breakfast, he dictated to Soult the basic data for some optimistic letters intended for Davout:

. . . the Prussians are withdrawing in disorder. Have a triumphal salute fired in honour of the victory. This is the moment to send us troops and to effect the raising of 200,000 men . . .

Baron Dominique Larrey, 1766–1843. During the Hundred Days he was Surgeon-in-Chief of the Imperial Guard. He was wounded and taken prisoner at Waterloo. By Pierre Guérin.

Colonel Sourd, Commander of the 2nd Chevau-Légers-Lanciers. At Genappe his right arm received six sword cuts and had to be amputated by Larrey. Although appointed general, he refused the rank in order to keep his command. Collection of Commandant Lachouque.

To Joseph:

The Emperor has just gained a complete victory over the Prussian and English armies . . .

Propaganda and imagination. Baudus, perhaps, and Flahaut certainly, coming from Gosselies, had given him an account of the battle of Quatre-Bras and read him Ney's report. In it, the marshal had deplored the "misunderstanding by Count d'Erlon that deprived him of a glorious victory . . ."

Despite which, in the order intended for the Prince of the Moscova, Napoleon dictated shortly afterwards:

The divisions acted independently: if the corps of Count d'Erlon and Reille had been together, not one Englishman in the attacking corps would have escaped (!). If the corps of Count d'Erlon had carried out the operation on Saint-Amand as the "Emperor had commanded", the Prussian army would have been completely destroyed.

Who was to blame? D'Erlon was in the vicinity of Saint-Amand, for Vandamme had signalled the fact. An imperial order could have launched his troops against the Prussian right.

Napoleon continued with his dictation. One learns:

The Emperor is going to the windmill at Brye. It is not possible that the English Army will be able to take action against you. If it were so, the Emperor would march directly upon them by way of Quatre-Bras while you launch a frontal attack with your divisions which, at present, must be reunited, and the British would be instantly destroyed.

Inform His Majesty of the exact position of the divisions and of all that is happening in front of you . . . His Majesty's intention is that you should take up position at Quatre-Bras, but if, by chance, that cannot take place, report immediately with the details, and the Emperor will go there himself just as I have informed you. If, on the other hand, there is only a rear-guard, attack it and take position.

The daylight hours of today will be needed to terminate this operation and complete the munitions, assemble the soldiers who have become isolated, and bring back the detachments. Give the consequent orders and make sure that the wounded are tended and sent to the rear.

Napoleon therefore did not contemplate continuing the military operations on that day unless he heard from Ney that the English were in strength at Quatre-Bras.

And indeed they were there . . .

Wellington, arriving at the crossroads at dawn, saw for himself that the French in front of him were alert – but what had become of the Prussians? Gordon, his aide-de-camp, sent off towards Sombreffe to look for them, was shot at, evaded some patrols and, on information from local people, finally

Mont-Saint-Jean, c. 1830.

The hamlet of Les Trois Burettes, where Napoleon gave the order to pursue the Prussians on 17th June.

The 7th Hussars in 1815. After Lalauze. Private collection.

The inn of La Belle-Alliance – the furthermost point to which the English rear-guard was pursued by Napoleon in person on 17th June. Private collection.

Napoleon entering Le Caillou. Marie Bouqueau, the farmer's daughter, watches the Emperor going into the building. By Count Louis Cavence, 1909. Collection of Commandant Lachouque.

The farm at Le Caillou before the battle. Napoleon's headquarters from 17th to 18th June. Collection of Commandant Lachouque.

found old Blücher at about 9.30 a.m. in a cabin at Mellery, lying in the straw, crippled with pain and giving Gneisenau his consent to order the retreat to Wavre.

"That's a good way off!" Wellington exclaimed when Gordon rejoined him under his shelter of foliage near the farm of Quatre-Bras and reported the news. "Old Blücher has had a damned good licking. Now he has gone ten miles back ... It will be necessary for us to do likewise. I suppose that in England they'll say we have been beaten ...but I cannot help it."

His decision was taken in the presence of the Prussian officer Massow.

"I am going to establish myself at Mont-Saint-Jean." (12 kilometres from Quatre-Bras.) "There I shall wait for Napoleon to give battle if I can hope for the support of even one Prussian corps; but if I am lacking that support, I shall be compelled to sacrifice Brussels and take up a position beyond the Escaut."

Enough to make the Prussian Command think things over!

The inn of Jean de Nivelles at Waterloo, where Wellington spent the nights of the 17th and 18th June and drew up and dated his victory bulletins.

116

So, on the morning of 17th June, the three commanders – almost at the same time – made decisions that were to determine the outcome of the campaign. Blücher and Wellington withdrew "to set the operations in order" – the first on Wavre and the second on Mont-Saint-Jean, with one detachment on Hal (Prince Frederick of the Netherlands).

Napoleon did not move and planned to spend the day putting his army in order.

This came as a disappointment to the troops. In the early morning the men had prepared soup, with water and the flour that was still in the sacks of those who would no longer need it, so that they would be ready to strike camp at dawn. And then they heard that the Emperor was going to inspect his regiments. Cleaning! Polishing! What was he thinking of? Soult was held responsible.

What was behind it? Drouet was alarmed. "The Napoleon we knew is no more," said Vandamme.

The Emperor left Fleurus in a carriage but was soon obliged to mount his horse because of the congestion on the road. At Ligny, Gérard was waiting for him. The houses were still burning under the bright sun; corpses that had been crushed under the wheels of vehicles were lying in the streets; the cemetery was a charnel-house; the church was a hospital; surgeons had been working throughout the night in surroundings that Dante might have created.

Waterloo Church, c. 1890.

The parish priest recited prayers and gave succour to the dying; his vicarage had been entirely devastated. The Emperor went by, consoling the wounded, distributing money. In a space smaller than the Tuileries Gardens, there were 4,000 dead.

Saint-Amand. And Vandamme presented to him a scene of chaos that was just as ghastly. General Girard had fallen here. Colonel Matis was now in command of his division, reduced to 2,000 men. Napoleon called to mind those who were missing: General Le Capitaine, veteran of the Spanish wars . . . the wounded – Habert, Maurin, Billiard, de Villiers, who had tried to prevent La Bédoyère from rejoining the Emperor; he had done his duty valiantly. Farine, Saint-Rémy, Vinot, so many others . . .

Now the procession ascended to the Bussy plateau cheered by the Guard, who were busy whitening their leather equipment. The veterans shouted so loudly that the Prussian cavalry guards near Tilly could hear them.

11 a.m. Near the tavern of Les Trois-Burettes, Napoleon dismounted and strolled around, talking about politics, about Fouché, about the latest news from Paris with his generals: Bertrand; Flahaut; Ruty, the inspector of artillery; Rogniat, commander of the engineers; Berge, Chief of Staff of the artillery; and others. In such a serious predicament, this freedom of spirit surprised but also disturbed his audience.

Then there was some news.

Grouchy confirmed the presence of a Prussian corps at Gembloux and sent General Berton's report.

Waterloo. Wellington's headquarters. Sketch by Captain Jones, from The Battle of Waterloo, *London, 1817.*

Ney wrote:

The enemy is presenting several infantry and cavalry columns that seem to want to take the offensive. I will hold out with Count d'Erlon's infantry and General Roussel's cavalry until the last, and I hope that I may even be able to repel the enemy until His Majesty lets me know his resolve. I will take up a position intermediate to Count Reille.

The troops referred to by the marshal would seem not to have been solely a rear-guard. An officer despatched on reconnaissance confirmed shortly afterwards the presence of English forces at Quatre-Bras covered to the left by a strong force of cavalry.

The Emperor decided to move against the English with his reserve.

Order to Ney:

Before Ligny, midday.

Marshal, the Emperor has just taken a position before Marbais with an infantry corps and the Imperial Guard. His Majesty has instructed me to inform you that his intention is that you should attack the enemy at Quatre-Bras to drive them from their positions and that the corps at Marbais will support your operations. His Majesty is proceeding to Marbais and awaits your reports with impatience.

Marshal of the Empire,
Chief of Staff, the Duke of Dalmatia.

At the same time, Napoleon gave Grouchy verbal instructions to go to Gembloux and pursue the Prussians: the corps of Pajol and Exelmans, Teste's division of the 6th Corps, and Vandamme's and Gérard's 3rd and 4th Corps were at his disposal. Written instructions would reach him later.

1 p.m. Grouchy, extremely worried about his mission, left the Emperor – whom he was never to see again – and made his way to Ligny to muster his detachment.

Napoleon arrived at Marbais, followed by the Guard and the cavalry under Domon and Milhaud. The 6th Corps and Subervie were there. Advance units moved towards Quatre-Bras; reconnaissance parties were sent towards Wagnelée and Villers-Perwins; but no one thought of sending even one patrol to the right, along the bad road leading to Tilly. And that was a great pity. Half the Prussian Army had secluded itself in this narrow corridor – tortuous, eneven, wooded – that wound across the scarcely-undulating plateau towards which marched Grouchy and his homologue, where Ney and Wellington already were.

Time was pressing. The Emperor was becoming impatient. Towards Quatre-Bras, dark clouds were banking up and there was a rumble of thunder.

But not the cannons . . .

Up came Marbot, colonel of the 7th Hussars. He had been at this position since the previous evening. His division (Jacquinot's) was at Wagnelée, with Durutte's division, left there on watch by the commander of the 1st Corps. His troopers, arriving at Marbais that morning, had confirmed that since 9 a.m. the British patrols had been more aggressive. They had taken a few prisoners, including a woman canteen attendant. She maintained that only the cavalry was at Quatre-Bras. The army had gone off in that direction – and she pointed towards Genappe and Nivelles.

The Emperor was beside himself. Wellington in retreat,

The Bodenghien Inn – Wellington's headquarters at Waterloo.

The village of Waterloo on 18th June 1815.

and this opportunity to crush the Army of the Low Countries slipping away . . .

When had the troops left? The last infantry and artillery had gone at about noon.

Blücher therefore had a start of fifteen hours over Grouchy; and Wellington had three or four hours start over Napoleon. Who could stop them joining forces?

The Emperor was already moving off towards Quatre-Bras; the artillery was under way; the 6th Corps was deployed, preceded by Milhaud's cavalry and followed by the Guard; Domon was on the right, and Subervie was on the left.

2.30 p.m. Buffeting wind, lightning, thunder. Lord Uxbridge, in command of the English cavalry, withdrew his squadrons towards Brussels. A battery endowed with fifty rounds enfiladed the Namur road . . .

The inaction of the French was certainly very odd.

But here they were now. The British gunners aimed badly. Under cover of the rain, the squadrons of Vivian and Vandeleur scampered off to Genappe. The Emperor pushed his cavalry after them.

At the crossroads there was no Prince of the Moscova. But no one should reproach him. Up to the arrival of the Emperor's last order, all the British Army that had been fighting the previous day was confronting him – not merely a rear-guard.

The Emperor gave vent to his wrath . . . the chance to defeat Wellington had been lost.

Torrential rain. On the Brussels road, transformed into a river, the lancers of Colbert and Subervie were virtually prodding the backs of Vivian's blue-jacketed hussars. The Emperor, drenched to the skin, was marching at the head of the vanguard of the 1st Corps.

At Gennape a few English batteries greeted the emergence of the pursuing 'pack', obliged to cross the Dyle over a bridge only 2½ metres wide. There was fighting on leaving the village. Colonel Sourd, commanding the 2nd Lancers, received sword cuts and lost his right arm. Surgeon Larrey operated on him by the roadside – after which, with clenched teeth and the stump stitched up, the colonel rejoined his regiment.

The march slowed down. Water swirled along the road, inundating the cavalry and artillery. In the fields, the infantry floundered in the mud and proceeded more slowly and in greater disorder than Grouchy's troops on their way to Gembloux.

The instructions dictated by the Emperor to General Bertrand, and sent to Marshal Grouchy in confirmation of the verbal orders given at Trois-Burettes at about noon, arrived:

Ligny. 3 p.m.
Rendezvous at Gembloux with the corps of General Pajol, the light cavalry of the 4th Corps (Vallin), the cavalry corps under General Exelmans, Teste's division, and the 3rd and 4th Corps. You will have a reconnaissance made in the direction of Namur and Maëstricht, and you will pursue the enemy. Reconnoitre his route and keep me informed of his movements so that I can fathom what he is going to do. I am moving my headquarters to Quatre-Chemins, where the British still were this morning. Our communication will therefore be direct by the paved road to Namur.

It is important to fathom what Blücher and Wellington are going to do and if they propose to cover Brussels and Liège in chancing the fate of the battle. Keep your two corps constantly together within a distance of two leagues.

Soult considered that Grouchy's detachment was too large. If the Prussians were now irrelevant, why launch a third of the army against them?

The marshal – uneasy, worried – would have preferred to operate near the Emperor. For the first time he was in supreme command; and under his orders were Vandamme, of the intractable nature, and Gérard – who had himself hoped for the baton of marshal.

Overpowering heat, a thunderstorm, torrential rain . . . and speed was essential.

Vandamme left Saint-Amand at about 1 p.m. At 3 p.m., under the driving rain, Grouchy and his staff were at Point-du-Jour; the head of the column of 3rd Corps was in sight.

Exelmans reported that the Prussians were at Gembloux "on the left bank of the Orneau". His men being worn out, the general limited himself to observing the enemy. The information was important: the Orneau, tributary of the Sambre, flowed through Perwès, Sauvenière, Gembloux and Mazy. If the Prussians were "to the left", it meant that they were to the north-west of this line.

At Point-du-Jour, Grouchy ordered Vandamme to march on Gembloux. The road had become a muddy stream. The pioneers preceded the artillery, which had become bogged down, and tried to help it get through. The infantry slid over the rye-grass, which had been trampled underfoot during the passage of the Prussians. With the men faring thus, it is possible to imagine how the cavalry, the vehicles and the duty waggons travelled . . . They laboriously covered no more than two kilometres an hour.

Point-du-Jour to Gembloux: two leagues. The head of the column of the 3rd Corps arrived at about 8 p.m.; the sun was setting as the advance posts were set up. The 4th Corps prepared its miserable bivouacs for the night in gardens and orchards.

On the evening of the 17th, the Coldstream Guards prepare to occupy the château of Hougoumont.

Reveille. Drawing by Job.

The information gleaned from the local inhabitants by the General Staff was, as is usual in such circumstances, confused and contradictory. The Prussians had departed – some towards Perwès, the others towards Wavre by way of Sart-à-Walhain. When the dragoons arrived at about 2.30 p.m., had they not seen Thielmann's infantry disappearing behind the curtain of mist? One brigade, sent to Sauvenière, had taken 400 head of cattle that would provide the soup for the evening meal; but contact with the enemy had been lost.

"Keep on the enemy's heels," Grouchy ordered. "Push forward six squadrons to Sart-à-Walhain and three to Perwès."

At about six o'clock, Bonnemains' brigade moved off in the rain.

7 o'clock. One of Pajol's officers reported that the Prussians were not retiring either to Liège or to Namur.

Squadron-commander Lafontaine, one of the marshal's aides-de-camp and of Belgian origin, had gathered the information taken from local inhabitants during a series of interrogations:

The enemy, 30,000 strong, continues to retreat in some disorder towards Wavre by way of Sart-à-Walhain. One column has taken the road to Perwès. All are asking the way to Brussels.

At headquarters, supper was eaten in haste. Grouchy was preparing the day's report for the Emperor.

After Genappe, Napoleon had lost the hope of overtaking Wellington.

At about 6.30, preceded by Jacquinot's cavalry and followed by the 1st Corps, he passed beyond the woods of Neuve-Court and arrived near a house on a height. It was called La Belle Alliance. Ahead of him, 800 metres away, Brunswick's black cavalry clattered around in disorder, trying to get out of a small valley traversed by the Brussels road and gain the scrub that stood out from the forest of Soignes and hid the approaches. The rain had stopped, but the mist was heavy and thick.

The Emperor ordered several guns of the 1st Corps to open fire on the outskirts of the forest. Full salvoes answered from the northern crest of the valley. On Le Capitaine's map, two names could be read: Mont-Saint-Jean and Waterloo.

Wellington's army had stopped there.

But for how long? The Emperor feared that he would see it disappearing into the forest, for the Duke would certainly not agree to do battle facing such a defile.

The night of 17th/18th June

Night fell. Napoleon personally settled the corps progressively as they arrived. "This was the first bivouac in the campaign," wrote Lieutenant Martin of the 45th of the Line (Marcognet's division). "One could scarcely sleep on account of the water, but there was plenty of talk about the operations. Everyone was the general and no one listened to anything, which gave rise to amusing conversations. Each bivouac fire was transformed into a political office. But this did not prevent wood from being flung on the fire, and the pot was kept boiling."

Napoleon set out in his second line – to the left of the road – the cuirassiers of Watier and Delort, of Milhaud's corps: 2,500 stiff apparitions in their light cloaks, soaked and mud-spattered. Generals and colonels huddled together in the farm at Monplaisir. To the right, Domon's chasseurs bivouacked in the mud with the helmeted lancers under Auguste de Colbert and Subervie's chasseurs. Jacquinot's cavalry covered the assembled troops ahead and to the right. Outside, the sentinels kept watch. The passwords were Biron, Brest and Bonté.

18th June. 12.30 a.m. At Quatre-Bras one of Grouchy's officers arrived from Gembloux by way of Sombreffe – a dreadful route. According to the information given the previous day by the Emperor to the Marshal, the Imperial Headquarters must be hereabouts. In the Bossu woods, the wounded were crying out: everything was sodden in the sultry atmosphere. Corpses of men and horses . . . On the road to Gennape, soldiers were marching in groups; further on, near the villages, flames from bivouac fires flickered here and there. At the roadside troopers were asleep on their feet, with their heads in their arms and their bodies leaning against their horses.

At Genappe, as soon as the bridge had been crossed, there were shouts as fatigue parties, servants, troopers and vehicles jostled and collided with each other. Generals Reille, Bachelu, Foy, Jérôme Napoléon and Piré were accommodated at the Hôtel du Roi d'Espagne. At supper, a waiter at the inn who had that same morning served breakfast to the Duke of Wellington said that one of the Duke's aides had spoken of a concerted link-up between the British and the Prussians at the beginning of the forest of Soignes. Hostelries were overflowing with officers from the 2nd Corps and 6th Corps, which were bivouacked in the orchards and woods of Ways, Boisy, Thy and Loupoigne. The generals' mess was at Plancenoit, and Marshal Ney lodged at Chantelet. The Imperial Headquarters was set up in a farm at Le Caillou, high on the slopes bordering the Brussels road, flanked by a sheep-fold, two barns and three stables that were drowning in the flooded greenery. A walled orchard that ran from the courtyard towards the north had already been commandeered as a bivouac for the duty battalion (the 1st of the 1st Chasseurs à Pied, under Duuring's command).

Along the road came the cavalry of the Guard and the vehicles of Captain Coignet, baggage-master of the Imperial Headquarters: the Emperor's sleeping coach, a landau upholstered in blue, and waggons carrying his papers, household effects, victuals, treasure, provisions and the like.

The servants prepared the Emperor's camp-bed in a small room on the ground floor, overlooking the road, and opened the luggage he required. There was a good fire in the grate. The valets – Ali and Neverraz – undressed the Emperor, who retired to his bed and had his supper there.

The first room on entering the building was reserved for the duty officers. In the rooms on the first floor were bales of straw for the 'Household' and the General Staff – of which the overflow would be sleeping on the stairs, in the barns and in the stables.

The Chief of Staff had not issued an order to halt; the divisions stopped of their own accord after having covered twelve kilometres in six hours.

There was chaos everywhere and pillaging for food . . . Someone was roasting a sheep; and, further away, a white colour was being burned . . .

It was one belonging to the 10th of the Line, and the incident began at one o'clock when General Jeannin, commanding a division of the 6th Corps and sharing a cottage with Colonel Roussel, overheard a discussion.

Paymaster Sabrier was saying, "Colonel, some time ago you were ordered to burn the old colour; and it is still in my baggage. If the men should see it, I would be massacred."

Jeannin, a veteran of the Egyptian campaign, bounded in. "What standard?"

After embarrassed explanations from the colonel, the general – in the presence of the Brigade General Tromelin and a police guard – did battle "for the colour" and burned the

emblem. But since Roussel could foretell the future, he kept the bow and tassel . . . which would be worth the stars to him . . .

Had they just burned, on the eve of Waterloo, the old emblem of the regiment of the monarchist colonel-general brought back from exile by the Prince de Condé (cf. Vicomte Grouvel, *Les corps de troupe et l'emigration française*)?

At Glabais, hunger drove the soldiers of the Guard to go marauding . . . Bivouacs became like clubs, discussions sometimes ending with the arguers drawing their swords.

The Old Guard grumbled that it all smacked of treason.

Le Caillou, 2 a.m. Grouchy's officer was stopped by the sentries. The Emperor read the despatches. The Prussians were not near Namur or Liège but were withdrawing either to Wavre or Perwès. The Marshal was having them followed.

On the whole, this was good news: Grouchy was taking care of the Prussians.

Reflecting the Emperor's thoughts, the Duke of Bassano wrote to the Duke of Vicenza:

The victory at Ligny is of the utmost importance; the élite of the Prussian Army has been crushed, the morale of that army will suffer the shock of it for a long time.

This was just what Wellington feared.

Installed in the course of the day of the 17th at Waterloo, in the inn displaying the signboard "à Jean de Nivelles", the Duke meditated for a long time. On the 16th he had lost 5,000 men and some of his most experienced commanders. His army was a mediocre military tool. But he did hold some trumps: his infantry was indefatigable, and his position at Mont-Saint-Jean was excellent. He had been familiar with it for some time, having gone over the ground, studying it in detail and discussing it with Colonels Pasley, Chapman and Carmichael Smith, and informing Lord Bathurst in 1814 that it could be advantageously utilised for halting a French invasion army. Bonaparte had allowed himself to be drawn into the net . . . That evening, Wellington went out to visit it again and also to encourage his "boys" and draw up his plans . . . not without experiencing some misgivings. Blücher was defeated, wounded; Gneisenau did not like him. Would Gneisenau harbour resentment because the British had not gone to the aid of the Prussian Army on the 16th? Would he come to their aid in the event of an attack by Napoleon? If so, he, Wellington, would wait for the French on the natural rampart stretching from Fichermont to Braine-l'Alleud; if not . . .

It was a plateau, of which the ridge running from east to west was intersected by the road from Charleroi to Brussels by way of Quatre-Bras, Genappe, La Belle-Alliance and Water-too. The ground sloped gently towards the forest of Soignes and more steeply to the south; at Mont-Saint-Jean it formed a junction with the Nivelles road. This ridge was approximately followed by a road coming from Ohain, bordered by a double quickset hedge, which formed a crossroads with the Brussels road – very overgrown, with banks measuring from three to five metres, and dominated by a large elm. This was the Chemin de la Croix – known as the "sunken road" after Victor Hugo had made it legendary. It was, in fact, sunken for a distance of 150 metres, after which it climbed upwards towards the west, flattened out, and finally reached Braine-l'Alleud.

Before this curtain there were three bastions – Hougoumont La Haye Sainte and Papelotte – and a wide and rather deep ditch formed by two small valleys, one running west towards Braine-l'Alleud and the other towards the east and the Ohain stream.

Beyond, there was a short ridge some 1,300 metres away in the region of that of Mont-Saint-Jean and appreciably nearer in the west. It was dominated by the red-roofed tavern La Belle-Alliance. Further away, to the south, the plateau curled into ridges and dales punctuated by small woods. The horizon was blocked out by the woods of Ohain, Paris and Chapelle-Saint-Lambert to the east and by the ridges of Braine-l'Alleud to the west.

Squatting on the ground under the elm tree at the crossroads, map in hand, Sir William Howe de Lancey, Quartermaster-General, gave Generals Constant, Lord Hill and Sir

Thomas Picton the orders for taking stations: they were to bivouac in their battle positions. The men were to eat, dry their clothes, and sleep. In the event of an attack, they were to resist from where they were.

Consequently, Chassé's division (6,000 men) was at Braine-l'Alleud and Merbraine; liaison to the left was with the British division under Clinton (6,000 men). Between Merbraine and the Nivelles road, in a T-shape from the principal line established along the Ohain road, were Cooke's division (the Guards brigade under Maitland and Byng), Ompteda's brigade and Kielmansegge's brigade. In the second line were Brunswick; three brigades of light cavalry under Grant, Dörnberg and Arjentschildt; Collaert's division and Lambert's British brigade.

Ample reserves were massed behind the right flank. The Duke particularly feared a manoeuvre by the French from that side.

The next to set up their bivouacs to the east of the road and in the shelter of the ridges, under the orders of General Sir Thomas Picton, were Perponcher's division, 2,000 English troops under Kempt, 3,500 Hanoverians under von Vincke and 2,000 Scots under Pack. Finally, towards Papelotte, were the Saxe-Weimar brigade and, in reserve around Vert-Coucou, the dragoons under Ponsonby including the Royal Scots Greys and the 6th Inniskilling Dragoons. Vandeleur and Vivian bivouacked on the outskirts of the forest. In principle, the auxiliary troops were encircled by the British brigades.

Wellington visits the British outposts in the forest of Soignes. Painting by Hippolyte le Comte. Apsley House.

D'Erlon's cannons interrupted the taking up of positions, provoking a reply from the Dutch artillery and panic among the waggon drivers, who cut the harness traces and galloped as far as Brussels, spreading confusion by shouting "The French are here!"

Returning to Waterloo, Wellington did some work and then went to bed.

There had been no news from Blücher.

Outside, the rain fell. The men could neither eat nor sleep, and they were wallowing in water. The Scots, shivering with cold, huddled together to keep warm. The horses turned their rumps to the rain and ate the soaked rye until they were full to bursting point.

All along the line of battle there was intermittent firing that tautened the nerves. It came from the infantry, who were discharging their weapons in order to clean them. As for the officers, without servants, baggage and supplies they could only wait for the sun to rise – at 3.48 a.m.

2.30 a.m. Wellington began working with De Lancey. He despatched pessimistic letters to the Governor of Antwerp, to the Duke de Berry and to his lady-love, Lady Frances Webster . . . "Be ready to leave Brussels for Antwerp in the event that this should prove necessary . . ."

There was also an order to Prince Frederick of the Netherlands to take up his position at Hal with the Anglo-Hanoverian division under Colville (17,000 men, 30 guns) to protect the army's right flank. He was forbidden to abandon the position without an express order signed by Wellington.

The day before, when refusing his aid to Blücher, the Duke had said, "I do not want to divide my forces." Why, then, on the morning of the battle did he deprive himself of the services of 17,000 men?

In a letter dated 8th December 1825, Mr. Littleton (Lord Hatherton) reported exchanges between the Duke and some of his friends concerning Waterloo. "I never intended to retreat to Brussels," Wellington is alleged to have said. "If I had been forced to fall back, I would have effected my retreat on my right, towards the sea, my ships, my supplies."

Gneisenau had his doubts . . .

"The English consider only their own interests," he said to Blücher, who was whining in his bed. "If they are beaten, the Prussian Army will run the greatest risks."

"To prevent this," replied the old warhorse, "we will have to help them."

3.30 a.m. A letter arrived from Wavre, datelined 1 a.m. In it, Blücher announced that he would be leaving at dawn and would attack the enemy's right flank with one or perhaps three army corps.

The Duke experienced an immense feeling of relief . . .

Day was about to break. In front of Dion-le-Mont, the vanguard of the 4th Prussian Corps (von Bülow) struck camp and made its way by the narrow, steeply-banked sinking lanes, marching raggedly, to Chapelle-Saint-Lambert.

The order from Gneisenau was: march slowly . . .

Panorama of the battlefield.

124

6. Waterloo 18th June 1815

At Waterloo, in front of the Bodenghien inn, the horses of His Grace the Duke of Wellington waited.

5 a.m. There he was – fresh, shaved, dressed in a uniform that had already become legendary: a small hat without gilt or plumes, a blue coat and a short cape. The Duke mounted Copenhagen, his favourite thoroughbred.

A moment later he was trotting briskly along the muddy road in the direction of Mont-Saint-Jean, accompanied by the Duke of Richmond and his son. He was followed by a group of horsemen: Müffling, Count Pozzo di Borgo, Lord Vincent and the Spanish General Alava among others; his aides-de-camp – Felton, Hervey, Lord Fitzroy Somerset, De Lancey, Gordon – and members of his staff.

It was a dull morning, but clear. In front of the farm of

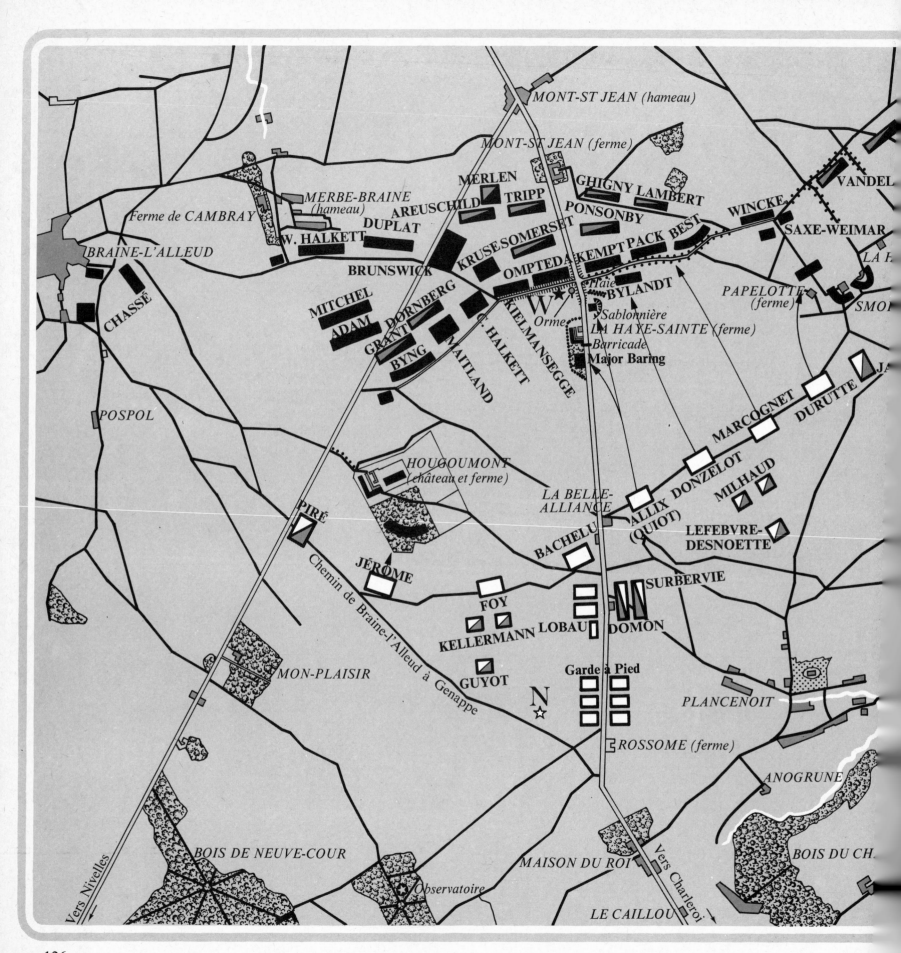

MONT-ST JEAN (hameau)

MONT-ST JEAN (ferme)

MERLEN

GHIGNY LAMBERT

VANDEL

MERBE-BRAINE
(hameau)

AREUSCHILD TRIPP

PONSONBY

WINCKE

Ferme de CAMBRAY

DUPLAT

SAXE-WEIMAR

W. HALKETT

KRUSESOMERSET

KEMPT PACK BEST

LA H

BRAINE-L'ALLEUD

BRUNSWICK

OMPTEDA

BYLANDT

PAPELOTTE
(ferme)

CHASSÉ

MITCHEL

DORNBERG

Haie

SMOI

ADAM

GRANT

C. HALKETT

KIELMANSEGGE

W

Orme

Sablonnière
LA HAYE-SAINTE (ferme)

BYNG

MAITLAND

Barricade

Major Baring

POSPOL

MARCOGNET

DURUTTE

JA

HOUGOUMONT
(château et ferme)

MILHAUD

PIRÉ

LA BELLE-
ALLIANCE

ALLIX DONZELOT
(QUIOT)

LEFEBVRE-
DESNOETTE

BACHELU

Chemin de Braine-l'Alleud à Genappe

JÉRÔME

SURBERVIE

FOY

LOBAU DOMON

KELLERMANN

MON-PLAISIR

Garde à Pied

PLANCENOIT

GUYOT

N

ROSSOME (ferme)

ANOGRUNE

BOIS DE NEUVE-COUR

MAISON DU ROI

Vers Charleroi

BOIS DU CH.

Observatoire

Vers Nivelles

LE CAILLOU

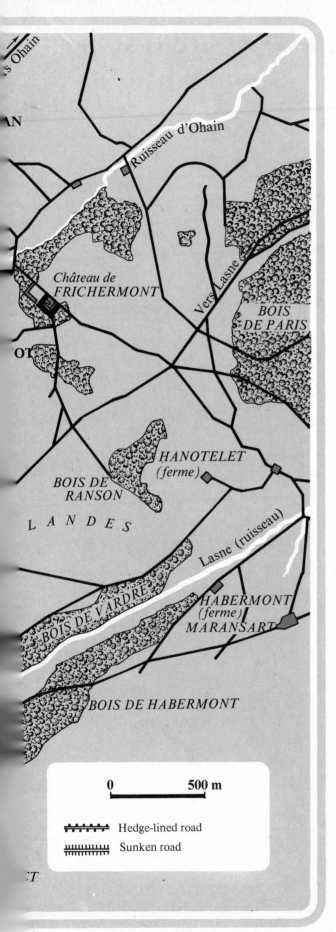

On the map: Ruisseau d'Ohain, Château de FRICHERMONT, Vers Lasne, BOIS DE PARIS, HANOTELET (ferme), BOIS DE RANSON, LANDES, Lasne (ruisseau), BOIS DE VARDRE, HABERMONT (ferme), MARANSART, BOIS DE HABERMONT

0   500 m

⊢⊣⊣⊣⊣ Hedge-lined road
⊢⊣⊣⊣⊣ Sunken road

Mont-Saint-Jean were some dismounted surgeons. Further away, the bivouacs had come to life. The soaked men, blue with cold and covered with mud, cleaned their weapons. Troopers groomed their wet and famished horses. Keeping the artillery carriages moving was laborious as they were filled with munitions and rum. It had been raining for fifteen days, and yesterday's storm had turned the roads into quagmires and swamped the rye-fields. The Duke was hailed, and then a prayer was said:

"May God take pity on our poor bodies."

The Prince of Orange was on the battlefield in the light blue pelisse embroidered with gold braid of the British 10th Hussars, of which he was honorary colonel. He wore a short cloak, and a hat with a white plume and a orange cockade.

Wellington having given his orders, the drums beat the call to arms and the troops took their battle stations as they had been trained to do in the Peninsular War: artillery and skirmishers in front; infantry behind, on the reverse slopes, hidden from view and artillery fire; the cavalry in reserve,

Waterloo: dispositions at commencement of the engagement (c. 11.30 a.m., 18th June)

On the French side: the strictly symmetrical dispositions for the battle. In the front line, Reille's corps to the left of the Charleroi road and Drouet d'Erlon's to the right of the road, both having cavalry protection and support on the flanks. In reserve, at the centre: Lobau's corps, Domon's and Subervie's cavalry and the Guard.

On the Anglo-Netherlanders' side: a strictly defensive position behind the Ohain road (sunken or hedged), with advance posts at Hougoumont, La Haye-Sainte, Papelotte, Le Haye and Frichermont but also with a right flank paradoxically abnormally extended, reaching as far as Braine-l'Alleud, as if Wellington feared the severance of his lines of communication, to the west, with the Channel – when it would seem that his main interest should have been to reinforce his left flank so as to avoid at all costs being separated from Blücher and thrust back away from the Prussians.

Panorama of the battlefield. In the foreground, Wellington's tree. Water-colour by an unknown artist. Musée Royal de l'Armée, Brussels.

The Duke of Wellington. By Sir Thomas Lawrence. Apsley House.

ready to step in. They would wait for the attack; and when the enemy, out of breath, approached the ridges the gunners would fall back to the next squares. The infantry would then disclose itself and open fire at close range. They would resist to the end . . .

The ground had been hastily prepared; a few trenches had been dug towards the rear. In front, the operational bases were manned and put into a state of defence:

To the right, Hougoumont. Woods. An orchard surrounded by walls and quickset hedges, farm buildings and the château: garrisoned by Colonels Macdonell and Saltoun, commanding four companies of Guards and one Nassau battalion – 1,500 men.

To the centre, the farm at La Haye-Sainte – solidly built, between an orchard to the south and a garden to the north: garrisoned by Major Baring, commanding the 2nd Battalion of the King's German Legion, reinforced by two Nassau companies. On the other side of the road, protected by an abatis and one battery, was Bijlandt's brigade (5 battalions) in the front line and one battalion of the 95th British in a gravel-pit.

The Prince of Saxe-Weimar's (Nassau) brigade occupied Papelotte and Fichermont.

The position, with good flank support and difficult of access, commanded extensive views and spread over 3,500 metres. Ready to defend it were 67,000 men and 156 artillery pieces. "I hope that all will go well," Wellington had just written to the Duke of Berry.

"The British oligarchy will be overthrown," said Napoleon. In the course of a reconnaissance that same morning he had been much encouraged on ascertaining that the British had not stirred – that their leader was going to do battle.

Optimism, therefore, on both sides.

On the bumpy road some small detachments proceeded, coming from Genappe – bundles of hairy mud, shouting "Long live the Emperor!"

At 9 a.m., having completed his review of the troops, Wellington, followed by his staff, dismounted near the elm at the crossroads and trained his telescope southwards.

French corps, their drums beating, were taking up battle stations.

At Le Caillou, Soult was dictating:

The Emperor orders the army to be ready to attack at 9 a.m. The commanders of the army corps will assemble their troops, see that weapons are in order and allow the soldiers to prepare a meal.

Was this possible?

No. As already explained, the waterlogged state of the ground was hindering the movements of the artillery. They had been through worse, and the mud was the same as that in which the British were floundering – but the troops had not all arrived.

The regiments had started out at daybreak; and then they had set up the cooking pots, and the wretched men had cooked flour mixed with water. No one on the General Staff had thought of ordering up the supply waggons, laden with bread, from the park at Charleroi . . . The 2nd corps passed in front of Le Caillou at about 9 a.m., followed by the Guard, Kellermann's cuirassiers and Durette's division of the 1st Corps. The 6th Corps did not leave Genappe until about noon.

The Emperor breakfasted with Soult, Maret, Bertrand, his brother Jérôme, Drouot, Ney and several generals in the small room next to his bedroom. They were served on silver plate. After the table had been cleared, the maps were spread on it and the Prince of the Moscova claimed that Wellington was in retreat. Soult expressed regret about the remoteness of Grouchy's detachment in view of its importance. Jérôme and Reille passed on the information given to them by the waiter at the Genappe inn about "a concerted link-up between the British and the Prussians coming from Wavre".

"Foolishness," retorted the Emperor. "After a battle like the one at Ligny, the joining up of the British and the Prussians is impossible. If my orders are carried out, we will sleep in Brussels tonight."

Why did they not do so?

Having ordered "a well-done shoulder of mutton" for supper, Napoleon mounted his mare La Marie and went ahead of the columns, stopping a little beyond Rossomme.

He had before him the complete panorama of the British position – concave, with the right flank thrown forward and the left flank refused.

It was a troop disposition for which the marshal had a liking.

Seated on the ground, two generals hastily scribbled the Imperial words detailing the order of battle:

Napoleon I. Artist unknown. Musée Royal de l'Armée, Brussels.

In the first line:

On the left: the 2nd Corps (Reille) from La Belle-Alliance to Monplaisir, 1,800 metres, 16,000 men, covered on the left by its cavalry (Piré).

On the right: d'Erlon's 1st Corps from La Belle-Alliance to Fichermont, 2,000 metres, 20,000 men.

In the second line:

On the left: Kellermann's cavalry, L'Héritier's dragoons and cuirassiers, d'Urbal's caribiniers and cuirassiers, 1 battery, 3,500 horse drawn up in two lines of formations.

In the centre: 6th Corps (Lobau) to the left of the Brussels road, 7,000 men.

The cavalry under Domon and Subervie on the right, 2,400 horse.

On the right: 2,800 cuirassiers under Milhaud, 1 battery; drawn up in two lines of formations.

In the third line, the Guard:

On the left: Guyot's reserve cavalry, 1,600 horse.

In the centre: the infantry in front of Rossomme, on each side of the road. Artillery behind the infantry. 12,000 men.

On the right: the light cavalry (Lefebvre-Desnoëttes), 2,000 horse.

When these troop movements had been completed, the French Army would be in a non-articulated geometric mass formation consisting of 72,000 men supported by 270 guns.

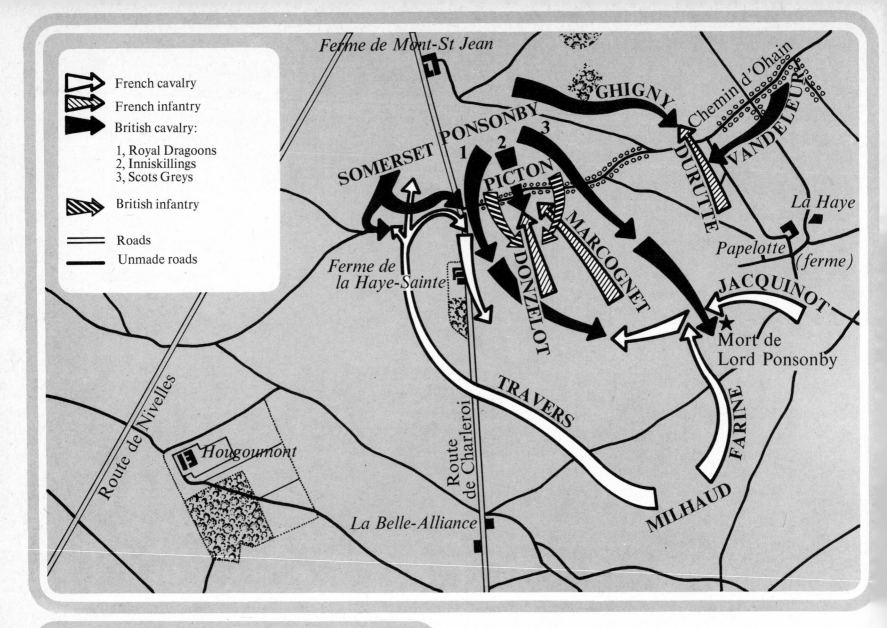

Legend:
- French cavalry
- French infantry
- British cavalry:
  1, Royal Dragoons
  2, Inniskillings
  3, Scots Greys
- British infantry
- Roads
- Unmade roads

Ferme de Mont-St Jean

GHIGNY

Chemin d'Ohain

SOMERSET PONSONBY

VANDELEUR

PICTON

DURUTTE

La Haye

Papelotte

(ferme)

MARCOGNET

Ferme de la Haye-Sainte

DONZELOT

JACQUINOT

TRAVERS

Mort de Lord Ponsonby

Route de Nivelles

Route de Charleroi

FARINE

Hougoumont

MILHAUD

La Belle-Alliance

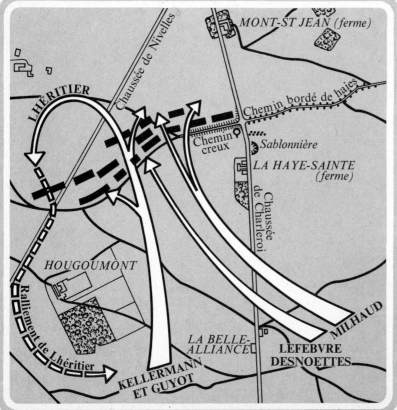

MONT-ST JEAN *(ferme)*

Chaussée de Nivelles

LHÉRITIER

Chemin bordé de haies

Chemin creux

Sablonnière

LA HAYE-SAINTE (ferme)

Chaussée de Charleroi

HOUGOUMONT

Ralliement de Lhéritier

MILHAUD

LA BELLE-ALLIANCE

LEFEBVRE DESNOETTES

KELLERMANN ET GUYOT

The battle of Waterloo: principal phases of the battle

1. The British Counter-Attack (at about 2.30 p.m.).
In order to check the infantry assault led by Drouet d'Erlon's corps against his left flank, Wellington had to crush Donzelot's division with Picton's infantry. To the west of La Haye-Sainte, the French cuirassiers of Travers, charged by Somerset's Household Cavalry, were overwhelmed in the sunken road and then flung back along the Charleroi road towards La Belle-Alliance. Ponsonby's dragoons forced Donzelot and Marcognet to retire in disorder, while the cavalry under Ghigny and Vandeleur charged Durutte's division. But venturing too far from their bases, the British dragoons were intercepted – on Napoleon's orders – by Farine's cuirassiers and Jacquinot's lancers. The British cavalry then had to regain its position to the north of the Ohain road.

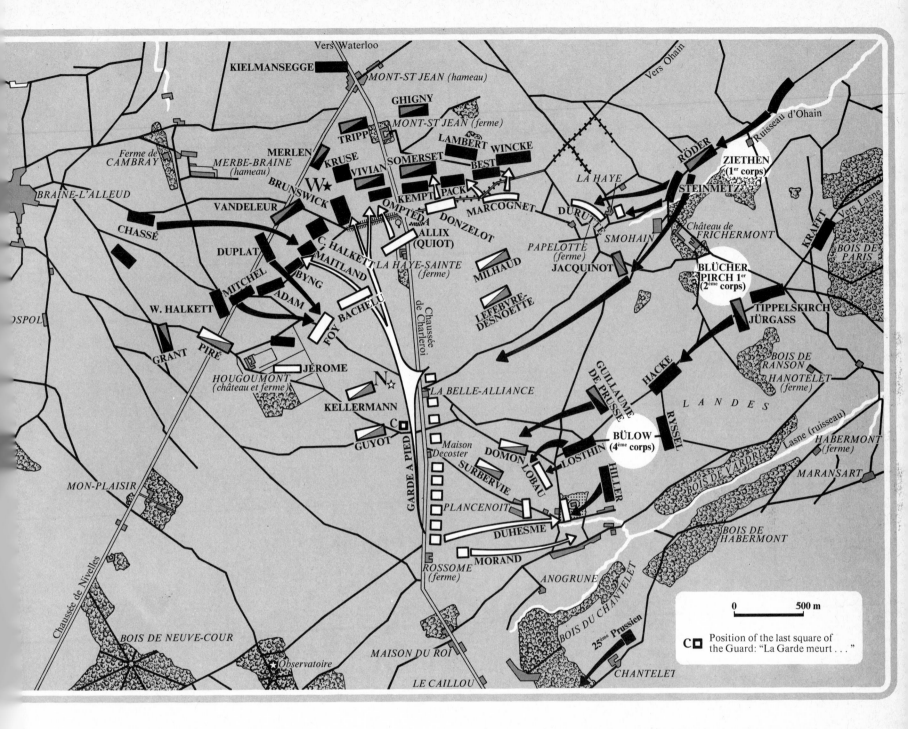

2. The Charges of the French Cavalry.

This map shows clearly the restricted zone of their impact on the British line: about 800 metres against the line's right centre. They were all developed in the sector between Hougoumont and La Haye-Sainte in order to avoid the sunken road as well as the hedged sector of the Ohain road.

The arrowheads indicate the average level of penetration of the Imperial cavalry squadrons between the Anglo–Dutch squares.

To illustrate this, the map shows the complete movement of l'Héritier's division (cuirassiers and dragoons) of Kellermann's corps, during the fourth charge. It had to cover almost 1.5 kilometres to reach the enemy lines, followed by a wheel of 2.7 kilometres (passing to the west of Hougoumont) to regain its base. Thus, for a single charge, it had to travel more than four kilometres.

3. The Battle of Waterloo, 18th June 1815, at about 7 p.m.

Napoleon was to make his final attempt to pierce the enemy front by calling up his last reserves. The battalions of his Garde à Pied were lined up in readiness on the right side of the Charleroi road. They would strike at the same point at which the great cavalry charges had been directed.

To resist the attack, Wellington did not hesitate to reinforce his centre by withdrawing troops from his left flank – safeguarded by the approach of von Ziethen's Prussian corps – and bringing Chassé's corps of Dutch-Belgian troops into the front line.

The right flank and the rear of the French Army were under direct threat of a breakthrough by Ziethen at Smohain and by Bülow's onslaught, backed up by Pirch, on Plancenoit. The Guard fell back – and Napoleon's army, half-encircled, gave in to panic and was routed.

From 11 a.m. to 3 p.m.

The château at Hougoumont and its outbuildings. The key outpost of the right flank of the Army of the Low Countries, it was defended by seven companies of the 1st and 2nd Coldstream Guards and by the British 3rd Regiment of Foot Guards, one Hanoverian company and the 1st Nassau Battalion. This garrison of about 1,500 men was commanded by Lieutenant-Colonel J. Macdonell.

Prince Jérôme Napoléon, 1784–1860, commandant of the 6th Infantry Division. Lithograph by Zephirin Belliard. Private collection.

The attack on Hougoumont

The troops arrived slowly and acclaimed the Emperor as they took up their positions. The British could hear the French bands playing "La Marseillaise" and the "Chant du Départ". 10 a.m. Napoleon was growing impatient; his right flank was restive . . . What if the waiter at the inn had been speaking the truth?

He ordered d'Erlon to send Colonel Marbot, with his 7th Hussars and a battalion, beyond Fichermont. Posts were to be set up at Coutures and at the Mousty and Ottignies bridges – possibly to try to make contact with Grouchy, to whom Soult had sent the following order:

His Majesty is going to attack the British army, which has taken up its position at Waterloo (?). His Majesty desires that you should direct your operations on Wavre in order to draw you to us again, put in touch with operations and link communications, driving before you the Prussian army corps that would have been able to stop at Wavre, where you must arrive as soon as possible. You will have the enemy columns engaged on your right flank followed by some light corps in order to keep them under observations and pick up their stragglers. The Emperor wishes to have frequent news from you.

(signed) Duke of Dalmatia.

Grouchy was at that moment at Walhain (7 kilometres from Gembloux), marching towards Wavre; and he had just sent Vincent's brigade (15th and 20th Dragoons) to Ottignies . . . Since morning, the Prussian majors von Falkenhausen and Wittowiski had been exploring the depths of the Lasne, but the French dragoons and the Prussian hussars did not run into each other . . . Such is life!

The Emperor thought about the Prussians, but he showed no intention of ordering Grouchy to the battlefield. He was,

The 1st Nassau Battalion disputes each foot of scrubwood at Hougoumont with Bauduin's infantry brigade. By Knötel.

however, annoyed at being obliged to again delay his attack on the British Army.

At about 11 a.m. he dictated to Soult:

Once the enemy is in battle order, at approximately 1 p.m., the moment the Emperor gives the order to Marshal Ney, the attack will be launched to seize the village of Mont-Saint-Jean. To this end, the 12-pounder batteries of the 1st, 2nd and 6th Corps (24 guns) will fire at the troops in Mont-Saint-Jean, and Count d'Erlon will launch the attack by taking forward the division on the left and supporting it, according to circumstances, with the other divisions of the 1st Corps. The 2nd Corps will advance proportionately to remain level with Count d'Erlon.

There is only one copy of this document in the French war archives. It mentions that the original bore a pencilled note, signed by Marshal Ney, that read:

Count d'Erlon will understand that it is on the left instead of on the right that the attack will begin. Pass on the information concerning this new arrangement to General Reille.

Without specifically stating it, this paragraph refers to the attack on Hougoumont – probably the subject of a verbal order . . . "It was only a question," wrote General Reille, "of keeping in the hollow, behind the woods, in support of a strong line of skirmishers in front."

The Emperor modified the plans for his offensive many times. At first the attack was to be on the centre and on the right with the 1st Corps, supported by 24 12-pounder guns,

grouped in a single battery on the ridge of La Belle-Alliance, and a decisive attack with the Guard – possibly the 6th Corps – all the cavalry, and the artillery reserve directed towards Papelotte in order to throw the British back towards the west and separate them from the Prussians.

The order dictated at 11 a.m. shows, however, that Napoleon had now abandoned all thought of manoeuvring in favour of a massive attack on the concave centre of the British line.

At about midday, everything was ready . . .

The defence of Hougoumont. Captain Jones, The Battle of Waterloo, *London, 1817.*

But what was happening on the plateau, between the Paris woods and Couture-Saint-Germain, towards La Chapelle-Robert? It was possible to make out something glittering . . . The field-glasses were trained in that direction. Perhaps a troop movement . . . French? Prussian?

Did the Emperor suspect it was the Prussians?

He sent his aide-de-camp General Bernard in that direction to learn the details: then he began to pace up and down, lashing the ground with his riding whip, stopping, looking now through his telescope . . . Obviously, this was what the waiter at the Genappe inn had meant . . .

A letter from Grouchy – headed "Gembloux, 6 a.m." but only just received:

All my reports confirm that the enemy is withdrawing to Brussels to concentrate there or to give battle after joining up with Wellington.

"Prussians at Mont-Saint-Guibert" General Milhaud had signalled yesterday.

Up came Bernard, hat in hand.

"What news?"

"Bad, sire."

"They are Prussians, aren't they?"

"Yes, sire."

"I thought as much."

The information was confirmed shortly afterwards by a prisoner belonging to the 2nd Silesian Hussars. His unit – the

Farm at Hougoumont. The southern gateway seen from inside the courtyard.

Lieutenant-Colonel Sir James Macdonnell, defender of Hougoumont.

Coldstream Guards. Colonel's colour.

4th Corps (under His Excellency Lieutenant-General von Bülow) – was at Chapelle-Saint-Lambert.

For half an hour the battle raged in the Hougoumont woods. Perhaps the Emperor wanted to tempt Wellington to withdraw his centre . . . and also protect his own left flank. In any event, Jérôme's battalion entered the wood: and Bauduin's brigade repulsed the defenders behind the wall of the orchard occupied by the Nassau and Hanoverian battalions. It was a fierce battle. Bauduin was killed. Jérôme held out. The cannon thundered with increasing force.

The chapel at Hougoumont as it is today.

Gardener's house at Hougoumont as it is today.

The defence of Hougoumont. Painting by Robert Gibb. At about midday, the French infantry managed to break down the gateway to the farm but were driven back by the British Foot Guards. Scottish United Services Museum, Edinburgh.

Defence of Hougoumont. The inner court-yard. To the right, the gardener's house. Painting by Hillingford.

Lieutenant Legros – nicknamed "L'enfonceur" (the smasher) – and his pioneers chop a hole through the door panel with an axe.

Attack on the gardener's house by the infantry of Jérôme Napoléon's division. Painting by E. Crofts.

Colonel de Cubières, commander of the 1st Light, who was seriously wounded during the attack on Hougoumont.

Gateway to the gardener's house, seen from the outside.

A handful of infantry of the 1st Light, who had succeeded in penetrating to the orchard, resist the British garrison to the last man. Painting by E. Chaperon.

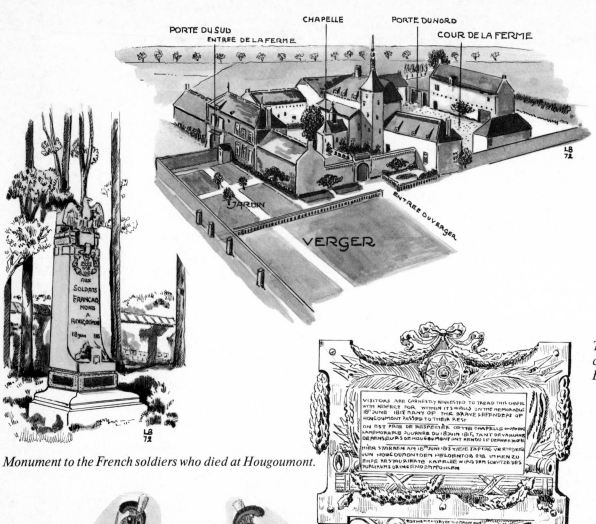

PORTE DU SUD
ENTRÉE DE LA FERME

CHAPELLE

PORTE DU NORD

COUR DE LA FERME

JARDIN

VERGER

ENTRÉE DU VERGER

Waterloo: Hougoumont château and farm before the battle.

This sketch – in perspective – gives a better idea of the scenes shown in the preceding pages. Emerging from the copse, the infantry of Jérôme Napoléon's division flung themselves against a wall pierced with loop-holes, through which their attack suffered heavy losses. They tried in vain to force their way through the southern gate. Driven back, they went round the west of the buildings and stormed the northern face. During the attack, Colonel de Cubières was wounded; and Lieutenant Legros managed to smash a panel in the gate, by means of which a handful of infantry of the 1st Light broke through – only to be exterminated by the garrison.

Monument to the French soldiers who died at Hougoumont.

Tablet placed on the wall of the chapel in 1907 by the British Brigade of Guards.

The crucifix of Christ in the chapel at Hougoumont.

British Household Cavalry.

1, trumpeter, Life Guards; 2, officer, Royal Horse Guards; 3, corporal, Life Guards; 4, officer, Life Guards; 5, trooper, Royal Horse Guards; 6, trooper, Life Guards. The British Household Troops included three regiments of cavalry – the 1st and 2nd Life Guards and the Royal Horse Guards.

Planche N°2

The appearance of Bulow's corps and Grouchy's dispositions

And Grouchy heard it. He was at the Marette farmhouse at Sart-à-Walhain (now called Walhain-Saint-Paul), home of the notary M. Hollert, who had invited him to breakfast.

Major de la Fresnaye had just left, taking a letter for the Emperor:

Blücher's 1st, 2nd and 3rd Corps are marching in the direction of Brussels. One corps coming from Liège has joined up with those that fought at Fleurus . . . This evening I am going to be in mass formation at Wavre and will find myself between Wellington, whom I assume to be in retreat before your Majesty, and the Prussian Army . . .

Grouchy was therefore proceeding to Wavre to attack the Prussians to whom Exelmans had drawn attention. Vandamme had reached Nil-Saint-Vincent.

The cannon thundered more and more heavily towards Mont-Saint-Jean.

General Gérard, commander of the 4th Corps, coming on ahead of his troops, presented himself to Grouchy and declared without any preamble that it was the Emperor's cannon they could hear and that they ought to march in that direction.

What happened in that green summerhouse (which today is no longer there)? Much has been written on the subject, but the conclusion is always the same: no one knows, because the accounts of the witnesses did not agree. It is only certain that Grouchy refused. The cannon were indeed those of the Emperor, who – as he had announced the previous day – was attacking the British. He had ordered the marshal to follow,

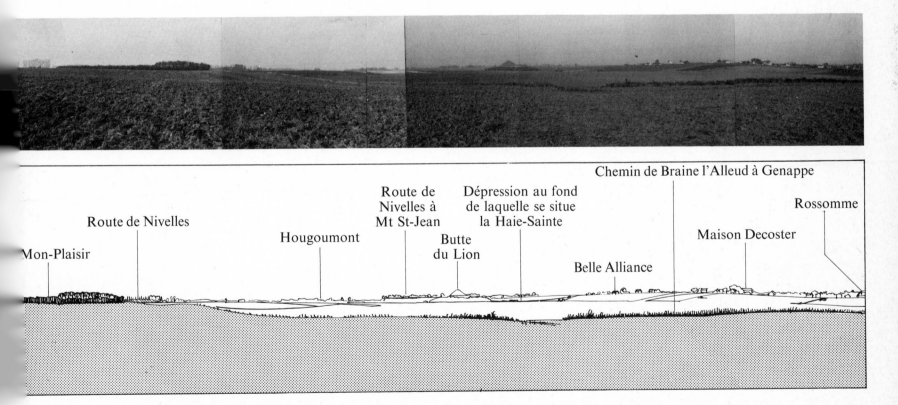

Diagram showing what Napoleon could actually make out from the heights of Rossomme. *The Emperor's field of observation was restricted – to his left by the Nivelles road, to the centre by a line roughly following the road from Braine l'Alleud to Ohain, and to the right by the Charleroi road. In these circumstances, even on horseback and using a field-glass, Napoleon could have perceived only the first British line and nothing beyond. Moreover, it was impossible for him to see what was happening to the east of the Charleroi road. It therefore seems arguable that the Emperor was able, from that position (as H. Houssaye writes), to see the heads of the Prussian columns emerging from Chapelle-Saint-Lambert. This would only have been possible if he had been situated near the Charleroi road, between La Belle-Alliance and the Decoster house.*

A non-commissioned officer of the Silesian 2nd Hussars, taken prisoner by Marbot's hussars, informs the Emperor that the Prussians under Bülow have arrived at Chapelle-Saint-Lambert.

General Gérard and General Vandamme beg Grouchy to march to the guns. By Philippoteaux.

Marshal Count de Grouchy, 1766–1847. On the 17th June Napoleon gave him the command of 33,000 men and 96 cannons. Collection of Commandant Lachouque.

watch, and attack the Prussians whom Exelmans had reported to be in strength at Wavre and on the left bank of the Dyle. Grouchy decided to carry out the order received – "march on Wavre and drive out the Prussians".

No one disobeyed the Emperor, and the war of initiative was forbidden to his officers.

Moreover, a letter dictated by Soult at this time confirmed Grouchy's mission:

You have written to inform the Emperor that you are marching on Wavre. This is in conformity with the dispositions sent to you by His Majesty. However, the Emperor commands that you must still manoeuvre in our direction so that you can rejoin us before a corps can get between us. The battle is engaged in front of the forest of Soignes.
P.S. A letter has been intercepted stating that General Bülow is to attack our right flank. We think we can glimpse this corps on the heights of Saint-Lambert. The enemy centre is at Mont-Saint-Jean. Thus you should manoeuvre to join up with our right.

Grouchy was a brilliant general. He was appointed marshal before the campaign began. At first Commander-in-Chief of the 4th Cavalry Corps of the Army of the North, on the evening of Ligny he was given command of an army corps with orders to pursue the Prussians and prevent them from joining up with the British. It would seem that the criticisms of him in respect of his conduct on the 17th and 18th June are in part unjust. His masterly retreat after Waterloo, which is so little known, did him great credit.

140

What a pity the Duke of Dalmatia did not suppress his letter and send only the postscript. How could Grouchy do battle at Wavre and manoeuvre towards Mont-Saint-Jean at the same time?

As it turned out, his letter – which was sent before 2 o'clock – did not reach its destination until between 5 and 6 o'clock. By that time . . . !

The Prussian menace was real enough. Bülow could arrive in front of Plancenoit in two hours, or two and a half hours at the most. Was the Emperor going to do battle on two fronts? He could still withdraw without risk, Grouchy reminded himself, and then manoeuvre according to his "system" to separate the two adversaries and destroy them one after the other. But to withdraw would be to beat a retreat . . . Could the sovereign, under the watchful eye of Paris, do this? What would they say – the critical middle-class, the Royalists in their fine lawn jabots, the writers of lampoons in the pay of Albion? Napoleon retreating . . . ! The candles in all the silver candlesticks in the suburb of Saint-Germain would be lit. "He is beaten!" would howl La Fayette, the liberals, the Chamber, his enemies.

Impossible! He must hold out, do battle and conquer . . . for the enthusiastic supporters who had acclaimed the triumphant salvo proclaiming the victory at Ligny; for the loud-mouthed fishwives with their cries of "Long live the Emperor!"; for the Fédérés des Faubourgs (the Royal communes) – all of these could be held in the grasp of glory . . .

"Napoleon had no time to spare for the drawing up of a new plan," Robert Margerit concludes. Pressed for time by

Marshal Count Gérard, 1784–1825, divisional general commanding the 4th Corps of the Army of the North. By Louis David. Collection of Commandant Lachouque.

Château de la Bavette.

La Marette farm, where Grouchy breakfasted on 18th June.

Lieutenant-General Count Exelmans, 1775–1852. commander of the 2nd Cavalry Corps. Collection of Count Exelmans.

The Dyle at Limale.

The battlefield of Waterloo. To the right of the Ohain road, the farm at La Haye-Sainte. Private collection.

the political unrest in Paris and throughout France, he needed not merely a victory but a brilliant victory . . .

Napoleon, who had dominated Europe, was going to stake everything on three square kilometres.

Namely, he would precipitate the attack against the British centre. This should take no more than one and a half hours if the thrust was vigorous and massive, led by the infantry, eight divisions of cuirassiers and a crushing artillery.

Accordingly, there would be an offensive show of force against Hougoumont by Reille with one division. The large battery would be reinforced by 8-pounders and some units of the Guard. An attack would be led by two divisions of the 2nd Corps and the 1st Corps on La Haye-Sainte and the British centre.

In addition, Domon's and Subervie's cavalry divisions would be sent towards the Paris woods to delay the march of the Prussians until the 6th Corps, proceeding later, could stop them.

Obviously, this would seriously reduce the reserves; and the blow to be struck against the British would therefore be less powerful.

An order to Marbot – who, ten minutes later, announced the presence of Grouchy and the Prussians in the Lasne valley – to make contact with the right flank by means of the outposts and patrols he had in that area. As a result of this, shortly afterwards a fierce combat took place in which Colonel von Schwerin, commander of the cavalry brigade of the Prussian 4th Corps, was killed. Marbot relates in his memoirs that Captain Eloy, stationed at the Mousty bridge, had sent out a reconnaissance party and did not fall back until about 6 p.m. Marbot could not have looked properly at his watch. If Eloy had been on the bridge later than 2.30 p.m. he would have been taken prisoner by the troops of the 4th Corps.

The latter were, in fact, already infiltrating the Paris woods . . . but with strict instructions not to reveal themselves. Blücher and, more especially, Gneisenau still did not trust Wellington.

1st Corps attacks

The 1st Corps, led by Marshal Ney, set off to attack the Anglo-Allied centre. Jean Augé, from Champ de Bataille de Waterloo *by L. Garros.*

Lieutenant-General Baron Marcognet, commander of the 3rd Division of the 1st Corps. Collection of Commandant Lachouque.

Lieutenant-General Drouet, Count D'Erlon, 1765–1844, commander of the 1st Corps. Musée de l'Armée, Paris.

Lieutenant-General Baron Quiot, 1775–1849, commander of the 1st Division of the 1st Corps. Collection of Commandant Lachouque.

143

The attack on La Haye-Sainte

Defence of the gateway at La Haye-Sainte. After W. B. Wollen.

The farm at La Haye-Sainte – solidly built, flanked by an orchard and a kitchen garden. This was the key point of the British line. The garrison, under the orders of Major G. Baring, consisted of the 2nd Light Battalion of the 2nd Brigade of the King's German Legion (five companies) reinforced by two Nassau companies. After the second French attack had been foiled, the garrison was reinforced by two companies of the King's German Legion.

The drama was to be played out between La Belle-Alliance and La Haye-Sainte.

Minutes were worth hours.

In Hougoumont, the show of power developed into a battle. Jérôme persisted; the combatants would stop at nothing less than a struggle to the death. Soye's brigade, called up in support, penetrated the woods; the battalion of the 1st Brigade – decimated by the Coldstream Guards taking cover behind the orchard walls – encircled the farm and the château in the west, and the 1st Light broke down the north gateway. There was slaughter in the courtyard, in the corridors of the château and in the chapel. The thatched buildings were set on fire; Jérôme was wounded. British tenacity and desperate French fury were at grips until evening fell, without Reille being able to influence the outcome and without the cannonballs being able to breach the wall in front of which the corpses were piling on top of each other.

Above, on the ridge of La Belle-Alliance, 80 guns of the 1st and 2nd Corps and of the Guard were firing two or three rounds a minute, creating a curtain of stagnant smoke under the intermittent light rain. The din was more terrible than the actual barrage. Situated 1,100 or even 1,400 metres away from the conflict, the guns were too far off to hit their targets – their fire barely reaching the reserve troops.

Why didn't the guns try to demolish La Haye-Sainte, which had been converted into a fortress? Or the orchard? Or the gravel-pit? All of these should have been attacked and taken…

Too late!

From the Papelotte crossroads, shouldering arms, shouting the "Chant du Départ", drums beating the charge, Drouet d'Erlon's four divisions, led by Ney, were mounting an assault on the British line. The eight battalions of each division were in line, serried in mass formation, one behind the other. It was impossible for them to deploy, to form squares, to shoot. Who had given the order for these Macedonian formations?

Marching between them came the divisional batteries: the 7th and 12th Cuirassiers (450 horse of Travers' brigade) supporting the operation to the west of the road.

Opposite them, Wellington – who was measuring his strength with Napoleon for the first time – looked on in astonishment. The five companies of the King's German Legion surrounded in La Haye-Sainte and the riflemen in the gravel-pit waited, finger on trigger. On the ridge, Bijlandt kept his Dutch troops under fire; but Picton made his Scots lie down, a little to the rear, in order to avoid it. Uxbridge gave the cavalry, under Ponsonby and de Ghigny, the order to mount.

Major Baring, commander of the 2nd Light Battalion of the King's German Legion, heroic defender of La Haye-Sainte.

Attack on La Haye-Sainte at about 1.30 p.m. Quiot's brigade (54th and 55th of the Line) of the 1st Division, after capturing the orchard, failed in its attack on the farm.

Colonel Baron von Ompteda, commander of the 2nd Brigade of the King's German Legion.

The two lines opened fire at the same time.

Quiot's soldiers stormed the orchard of La Haye-Sainte but could not demolish the walls with the butts of their muskets. One battalion surrounded the building. Wellington threw in some of Ompteda's battalions in support and they were immediately charged by Travers' cuirassiers, who drove back the skirmishers under Kielmansegge. Around Wellington, officers were falling: Lord Vincent and Count Pozzo di Borgo were wounded.

To the right, in the smoke, Donzelot and Marcognet, slightly screened by a dead angle, were approaching from the de la Croix road. Durutte made his entry at Papelotte.

Cavalry were needed.

Out of breath, slow to deploy, the divisions endured the fire from Kempt's line, followed by bayonet attacks. General Picton was killed; a colour of the British 32nd Regiment of Foot was taken. The 25th French, under Marcognet, bounded on to the plateau . . . Victory . . .

But they had to fall back, crushed by Pack's salvoes and charges. Forming then a confused mass, the centre battalions were shot down. And put to the sword.

Death of General Picton. Coloured engraving by M. Dubourg, after J. A. Atkinson. Private collection.

Right: *cavalry charge. Lord Uxbridge leading the charge of the 15th Hussars. Detail from a painting by Denis Dighton. Collection of the Marquess of Anglesey, Cooper Bridgeman Library.*

The British cavalry charge

Wellington gives the order to charge to Lord Edward Somerset. Behind and to the left, Picton is carried from the battle-field mortally wounded. To the right, the Household Cavalry Brigade prepares to charge. After a painting by A. Cooper.

Eagle of the 45th of the Line.

Charge of the Scots Greys. Sergeant C. Ewart seizes the Eagle of the 45th of the Line. Painting by Denis Dighton. By gracious permission of H.M. the Queen.

149

Wellington gives the British Army the signal for the general attack. Water-colour by J. A. Atkinson. British Museum, London.

The cuirassiers of Travers' brigade (7th and 12th Cuirassiers) charged by the 2nd Life Guards. Somerset's brigade was broken and thrown back to the Mont-Saint-Jean plateau. After a painting by Christopher Clark.

Left: *General Lord Edward Somerset, 1776–1846, commander of the Household Cavalry Brigade. By Jan Willem Pieneman. Apsley House.*

Sir William Ponsonby had just removed his dragoons, who had clattered down the slope shouting "No quarter!" and had overthrown the French forces under Quiot, Donzelot and Marcognet. The French columns, driven into a herd, were cut to pieces without being able to manoeuvre or even fire; they were swept away and put out of the fight. The Eagle of the 45th of the Line was captured by a sergeant of the Scots Greys; that of the 105th was taken by a corporal of the Royal Dragoons. On the left, the Guards Brigade overthrew Travers' cuirassiers but were in turn decimated by fire from the flank of Bachelu's division. Two out of four colonels were killed.

The British cavalry charge

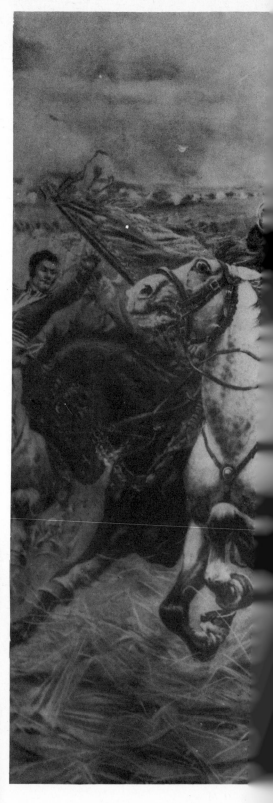

The Scots Greys cut down the gunners and drivers of two divisional batteries encountered during their charge. Painting by Henri Dufrey. Radio Times Hulton Picture Library.

The 92nd Gordon Highlanders and the Scots Greys. Painting by Stanley Berkeley. Reproduction in Scottish United Services Museum, Edinburgh.

The Earl of Uxbridge, Marquess of Anglesey.

Despite the sounding of the assembly by the trumpeters, the Scots Greys continued their charge and put two divisional batteries to the sword before being annihilated in a flank charge by the 6th and 9th Cuirassiers (Farine's brigade), sent in by the Emperor, and Jacquinot's lancers. Ponsonby was killed.

3 p.m. The attack of the 1st Corps, unsupported by the cavalry, failed.

"Thank you, gentlemen," said Wellington, raising his hat in front of what remained of the cavalry. His left flank had suffered; the murderous artillery fire to the east of the road was demoralising to the whole of his line. But his army had to hold on under pain of being destroyed.

Reille's corps had not marched abreast of the 1st Corps. Jérôme and Foy were fighting in Hougoumont; Bachelu was not in action.

A kind of mist mixed with smoke veiled the confusion.

Mounted on La Désirée, his fine grey mare, the Emperor traversed the battlefield where d'Erlon's divisions were rally-ing. Eight hundred British dragoons slain! Cannonballs rained down. General Desvaux de Saint-Maurice was cut in two by a missile while at Napoleon's side.

Towards the right, the Emperor could see that the Prussians were waiting expectantly . . .

Ahead, Quiot's and Donzelot's battalions were attacking La Haye-Sainte once again. It would be necessary to support them with a full and rapid action in mass formation . . . Perhaps there was still time to pierce the English centre.

Charge of the Scots Greys on the square of the 45th of the Line. Picture by Le Blant, from Au Drapeau.

Major-General Ponsonby, commander of the 2nd Cavalry Brigade (Royal Dragoons, Inniskilling Dragoons and Scots Greys). Artist unknown. National Army Museum, London.

The Eagles of the 45th and 105th of the Line being presented to Wellington. Engraving by Vinkeles, after the picture by Van Bree. Musée Royal de l'Armée, Brussels.

Two Imperial Eagles were lost at the beginning of the battle, the dispositions for attack of Drouet d'Erlon's corps rendering the infantry incapable of defending themselves against the British cavalry charges. Despite the ensuing rout, all the other Eagles were saved.

Wellington watched the French positions anxiously. Müffling reported that Blücher's troops were on the march; but when would they go into action? Men were falling right and left. File-closers bawled out "Close ranks!", "Aufgeschlossen!", "Serrez les rangs!"

At about 3.30 p.m., the Duke perceived through the smoke a large-scale enemy cavalry movement.

"Scotland For Ever". Charge of the Scots Greys. Painting by Lady Butler. Leeds Art Gallery.

General Bro de Commère in the uniform of a captain of the 7th Hussars. He became colonel in 1815 and commanded the 4th Chevau-Légers, at the head of which he recaptured the Eagle of the 55th of the Line.

Eagle of the 105th of the Line captured by the 1st Royal Dragoons.

The Rossomme heights, to the left of the Mont-Saint-Jean road at Nivelles.

A sunken road. The legendary sunken road has disappeared, the uneven ground having been levelled after 1815.

Major-General Viscount Farine, commander of the 6th and 9th Cuirassiers. Musée de l'Armée, Paris.

Final episode in the charge of Ponsonby's brigade. The Scots Greys – at the head of which can be seen General Ponsonby, who was killed instants later – receive a frontal attack from General Farine's cuirassiers and a flank attack from the lancers under Colonel Martigues. Painting by Charretier.

From 3p.m. to 7p.m.

The French cavalry attacks

The Emperor had just given Ney his cuirassiers.

Before the hurricane that was coming up briskly through the green rye, Wellington hastily reinforced his line with Mitchell's and Adam's brigades – drawn up to the rear on the opposite slope in sixteen squares in chessboard formation – called up Chassé's division and ordered the artillery to load the guns with grape-shot.

The cavalry were in agreement with Ney: neither the terrain nor the timing was right . . . Milhaud's twenty-four squadrons were obliged to traverse 1,000 metres of heavy ground encumbered by soaked crops standing three feet high before coming to grips with the waiting enemy.

What was to be done? There was only one answer – the cuirassiers.

The salvation of France was at stake. "The Emperor is counting, to effect a victory, on the energy of the Prince of the Moscova."

The situation defies description. Ney, the "Rougeaud", was let loose. Milhaud's divisions, drawn up in a line of columns of squadrons, trotted up the slopes of the British line. Among them was the cavalry of Wathier de Saint-Alphonse – the man of Wertingen, of Schleiz, of Friedland: and that of Delort – colonel at Austerlitz, scarred with wounds in Spain.

In the second wave came the light cavalry of the Guard. Who had given them the order?

The combatants were shaken by the madness of despair. The war had been going on for twenty-three years, and now the day of reckoning had arrived. One had to kill as many as possible before being killed oneself.

The French artillery stopped firing. And that of Wellington spat out short-range case-shot, grooving furrows through the squadrons that dashed up in disorder, their horses winded.

General Kellermann, Count Valmy. Private collection.

On the plateau there were bloody struggles followed by hand-to-hand fighting in an attempt to pierce the devilish squares formed to a depth of four ranks. Their passion for the fight was intense. Colin Halkett, Kruse and Maitland suffered but resisted. Lord Uxbridge hurled in the cavalry under Dörnberg, Arentschildt, Brunswick, Ghigny and van Merlen. Homeric conflicts took place, during which some squadrons charged ten, twelve, fourteen times.

159

Lieutenant-General Count Lefebvre-Desnoëttes, 1773–1822, commander of the Light Cavalry of the Old Guard. Collection of Commandant Lachouque.

General Baron L'Héritier, commander of the 11th Division, 3rd Cavalry Corps. Collection of Commandant Lachouque.

Brigadier-General F. Lallemand, 1774–1839, commander of the Chasseurs à Cheval of the Guard. Collection of Commandant Lachouque.

Did Napoleon say "It is too soon by one hour, but it is necessary to stand by what has been done"?

Be that as it may, he had ordered Ney to take his cuirassiers. And the Prince of the Moscova and Milhaud needed some time to form these twenty-four squadrons. Napoleon had seen the preparations . . . an aide-de-camp, at a gallop, could have held back the two divisions in the process of being assembled.

Flahaut was now making his way to the left to carry to Kellermann and all the cavalry the order "to support and follow those who have already passed the gully".

It was about 5 o'clock.

As the Comte de Valmy was not at the head of his corps, the aide-de-camp conveyed to L'Héritier, commander of the leading division, the Emperor's order to join the battle in strength. Wounded in every battle from Marengo to Znaïm, the victor of Brienne and Valjouan, L'Héritier dashed off with

Chevau-Légers-Lanciers reconnoitring for a body of cuirassiers. By Detaille. Musée de l'Armée, Paris.

This and the following seven pages show details of a fresco by the military painters Robiquet, Malespina and Desvarreux, under the directions of Demoulin. The work measures 110 metres in circumference and 12 metres in height. Forming a panorama of the battle, the fresco is in a circular building on the battlefield. Musée du Panorama de Waterloo. Photograph by Mallinus.

An episode in the charge of Guiton's brigade.

The French cavalry charge

Marshal Ney, followed by his aide-de-camp Colonel Heymes and by his staff, leads the charge of General Donop's cuirassiers (2nd and 3rd Regiments). General Delort's division of cuirassiers is in the second line.

In the foreground, charge of the dragoons of the Guard. To their right, the cuirassiers of General Vial. Behind are Farine's brigade and General Piquet's brigade of dragoons (2nd and 7th Regiments). In the background, the line of poplars that connected Hougoumont with the Saint-Jean-Nivelles road.

L'Héritier's division takes a horse artillery battery on approaching the squares of the second British line.

Charge of the lancers of the Guard, led by General E. De Colbert. To the left, in the foreground, the cuirassiers of Dubois' brigade (1st and 4th Regiments). Behind and to the left, La Haye-Sainte – in flames – and its orchard.

169

In Plancenoit, in flames, the Imperial Young Guard and the 1st Battalions of the 2nd Grenadiers and 2nd Chasseurs were overcome after a day of fierce fighting in an attack by the divisions of Hiller, Ryssel and Tippelskirch.

171

his eight squadrons of dragoons and ten companies of cuirassiers. Flahaut then joined up again with Kellermann, who immediately bristled. Madness! The little hollow of La Haye-Sainte was already overflowing with Milhaud's cuirassiers in disorder. To throw twenty-five fresh squadrons into the heap would mean presenting them to the enemy like poultry ready for the plucking.

Too late!

Furious, Kellermann took himself off at a gallop after his subordinate, catching up with him. They talked in the saddle, boot to boot . . . but it was impossible to stem the flood. The men would certainly not obey an order to halt. Cannily, L'Héritier made full use of the small dales that snaked between Montplaisir and Hougoumont. The division then approached the ridge of La Belle-Alliance and deployed in the gully. The survivors of Milhaud's forces profited from the clash and formed up behind them.

Further to the left, a section of Roussel d'Urbal's division emerged. Enraged to see his magnificent cavalry being squandered, Kellermann kept Blancard and his carabiniers pinned down with strict instructions not to enter the fight without an order from him. It was necessary for Guyot to come to a standstill with the cavalry of the Guard . . . but he had been ordered by the Emperor to charge. What should he do?

The squadrons took the valley that skirted Hougoumont and deployed to the left on reaching the crest in order to direct their attack against the British right.

The heat was overwhelming.

And to the right, the cannon thundered in the distance.

In the clearing at Beauchêne, the head of the column of the 4th Prussian Corps, supported by the four batteries, emerged from the Paris woods. Judging Wellington to be sufficiently engaged, Blücher had just ordered Bülow to come out of cover and attack the French right flank in the direction of Plancenoit.

Domon's and Subervie's cavalry, soon overwhelmed, fell back to the rear of the 6th Corps.

At about 5.30 p.m., after several attacks, Lobau withdrew to Plancenoit, where the struggle became epic.

Bülow had 30,000 men and 80 guns. Behind him was Pirch I with 20,000 men.

Facing them were the 6th Corps and two cavalry divisions, consisting of 8,500 fighting men and 16 guns.

Would they be able to hold out?

The village was a nest of cannonballs. The Prussian projectiles were now reaching the Charleroi road and falling on

Left:
Charge of the 11th Cuirassiers (Guiton's brigade) on the Nassau squares of General Kruze.

Major-General Halkett, 1774–1856, commander of the British 5th Brigade. By Jan Willem Pieneman. Apsley House.

Major-General George Cooke, 1766–1837, commander of the British 1st Division. He was wounded at the end of the charges by the French cavalry. By Jan Willem Pieneman. Apsley House.

The Lanciers-Rouges at Waterloo. Drawing by Job, from La Vielle Garde Imperiale. *Éditions Mame.*

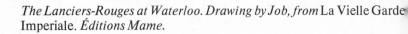

the squares of the Guard. Here, too, was to be found the courage born of despair . . . "No quarter!" bawled the Scots Greys. "No quarter!" took up the Prussians, like an echo of the "No prisoners!" hurled out on the evening of Ligny by General Roguet, second-in-command of the Grenadiers à Pied.

Fight to the death . . .

The Emperor ordered the Young Guard, under Duhesme, to move to Plancenoit and go into action on the right of the 6th Corps.

Hold out at all costs . . .

The reserves were dwindling . . . Almost the entire French Army was fighting at odds of one to three. There was no hope of further assistance. Unless Grouchy . . .

But Grouchy was in front of Wavre, grappling with the 3rd Prussian Corps. The position he had been ordered to take was strongly held; the corps under Vandamme and Gérard were making headway with difficulty.

General Count Edouard de Colbert, 1774–1853, commander of the regiment of Chevau-Légers-Lanciers of the Guard. Wounded on the 16th he led the charge of his cavalry with his arm in a sling. Painting by Dubois. Musée de l'Armée, Paris.

Colonel Major Baron Jermanowski, commandant of the squadron of Polish Chevau-Légers of the Guard, who went with Napoleon to the Isle of Elba. He was wounded at Waterloo at the head of his cavalry. (During the Hundred Days, this Polish squadron, with its 109 troopers, was incorporated in the Red Lancers of the Guard). Bibliothèque Polonaise, Paris.

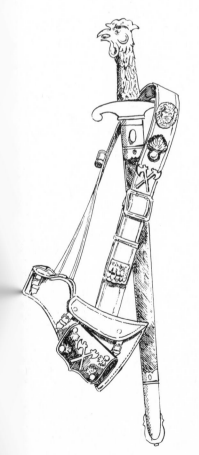

Charge of the Belgian 2nd Regiment of Carabiniers. Painting by Alphonse Lalauze. Musée Royal de l'Armée, Brussels.

The last trophies. Painting by Chaperon. Roger Viollet.

During their charges, the French cavalry captured several colours. The number is given as six by Thiers (Le Consulat et l'Empire) and by General Regnault. General Delort, in his account, refers to an English colour being seized by a quartermaster-sergeant of the 9th Cuirassiers and that of a battalion of the King's German Legion by Captain Klein de Kleinenberg of the Chasseurs of the Guard. The regimental history of the 10th Cuirassiers mentions an English standard captured by Sergeant Gautier.

42nd Highlanders. Regimental Colour.

The British in difficulty

6.45 p.m. The sound of the cannon from Mont-Saint-Jean seemed less powerful.

True. From the high ground of La Belle-Alliance, the Emperor looking towards La Haye-Sainte. The cavalry charges were ending in dreadful agony in the valley below. Ney, hatless, dripping with sweat, regrouped a few cavalry units and launched them once more into the fray.

The successive impacts finally overwhelmed the British squares, some of which collapsed and dispersed. That of the 69th was cut to pieces. Colin Halkett suffered eleven charges; Alten's infantry was worn out; Adam and Cooke were wounded. Lord Hill, bareheaded, encouraged his men to endure. Wellington was everywhere – not speaking to anyone but, with that nervous idiosyncrasy peculiar to him, feverishly playing with his field-glasses. "Stand fast," he told the 95th. "What would they say in England if we were beaten?"

He very nearly was.

The next day he was to write to Brussels: "It was the most desperate business I ever was in. I never took so much trouble about any battle, I was never so near being beat."

Broken and dislocated, the Army of the Low Countries was exhausted. The French cuirassiers, who had been able to maintain themselves on the plateau with infantry support, had penetrated the enemy squares and carried off six colours. The 8th had galloped right up to the convoys in the midst of cannonballs and shot from the reserve batteries, spreading panic among the rear troops before wheeling to the left and attacking the British front line from the rear with sword in hand and then rallying to the south of Hougoumont. Their colonel was wounded. Eleven cavalry generals were hit; two were killed. Three hundred officers were disabled.

The Battle of Waterloo. W. Pieneman. Rijksmuseum, Amsterdam.

Plancenoit

"Gentlemen," Wellington was to say later, "the best cavalry in Europe is the French cavalry. I know something about it."

Between the ridges of La Belle-Alliance and Mont-Saint-Jean, the terrain had truly become a valley of death. Ten thousand of Wellington's men reached the forest of Soignes. "Many soldiers," he was to say, "considered their presence indispensable where there were no more shots to be received."

An order from the Emperor was awaited – some tangible sign of his military genius; the order that would set the last battalions in motion. The British front had been thrown into such confusion that it could be pierced . . . if action were taken quickly.

Ney called up Bachelu and one brigade of Foy's division. But the operation was not carried through instantaneously. It took time for the generals to form the regiments into divisional columns, to cover the 1,500 metres of quagmire . . . and it was too late. Wellington's artillery had found new courage. "It is a hail of death," said Foy, wounded.

However, the impetus had been given and the infantry went at the British with their bayonets. One brigade, withdrawn from Durutte's division, did battle to the east of La Haye-Sainte. The attempts failed; but twenty precious minutes had been gained, and the Emperor gave the order to try the breakthrough towards the crossroads.

At the head of the 13th Light and a detachment of the 1st Engineers, Ney flung himself against the walls of La Haye-Sainte and took the farm from Baring's light infantry. One horse battery, brought to the vicinity, opened fire at a range of 200 metres on the British, whose guns, horse-teams and gunners were overthrown. To the right, the remnants of the 1st Corps pressed forward.

"The centre of the line was open," von Alten was to state. "We were in peril," wrote Kennedy, Wellington's aide-de-camp. The objective was reached. The British gave way. The rear areas were filled with fugitives . . .

Victory beckoned to the Emperor.

Now it was the right flank that cracked.

Lobau, overwhelmed by sheer weight of numbers, withdrew his left flank. Duhesme called for support. The Emperor backed this up by sending General Pelet, commander of the 2nd Chasseurs à Pied of the Old Guard, at the head of two battalions (600 chasseurs and 600 grenadiers). Pelet, on horseback, was in his shirt-sleeves. On skins made slack by rain and sounding dull and hollow, the drummers beat the charge: the veterans, in close columns by half-companies, drove the Prussians back to their batteries.

Colonel von Stülpnagel, commander of the 12th Brigade of the 3rd Prussian Corps.

By dusk, on this day of mammoth conflict, the French ended up victorious on all sides. With the British smashed and the Prussians driven back, it needed now – somewhere – the finishing stroke . . . This partial success must at least be exploited before the entry into the line of the 2nd Prussian Corps, whose rearguards could not be very far from Pajol's hussars sent by Grouchy.

But the marshal's infantry had only reached the high ground of Rixensart as night fell.

La Belle-Alliance. 7 p.m. The combatants were out of breath; British cannonballs were less frequent. Amid the stagnant smoke, there were shouts, galloping, firing from the platoons. In the area of Plancenoit, Pelet had passed beyond the village. The Young Guard advanced; Lobau's infantry no longer fell back.

Hougoumont was in flames, but the British still held on. Some of Prince Jérôme's companies encircled this key point. Piré signalled that a column was coming from Braine-l'Alleud: it was Chassé's division, called to the centre by Wellington.

To the east, it was not known if Durutte occupied Papelotte.

Straight ahead, the survivors of the 1st Corps – gathered together by d'Erlon and launched once more by Ney – approached the ridges, bristling with Scots. The 6-pounder battery brought up at a gallop by the marshal fired with intention of demolishing the battalions of Ompteda, who had just been killed. The 5th fell back. The 8th lost its leader and a colour: only thirty men were still standing. The 6th Dragoons and Sir John Lambert's brigade, sent to the crossroads, had already been decimated. There remained only 140 of von Arentschildt's hussars, two meagre squadrons of the Guards, and one squadron of Ponsonby's brigade. Wellington ordered the Foot Guards to fall back behind the natural cover afforded by the terrain. Munitions were running low: eighty pieces of artillery of all nationalities were now silent, abandoned, muzzles overheated.

Ney, unshaven, his sword broken, scoured the plain, assembling all who could walk or ride. One last effort. They are curs . . .

Shot followed shot . . . The Prince of Orange, Alten, Kempt and Fitzroy Somerset were wounded; Gordon and De Lancey were mortally hit. Kielmansegge retreated; so did Kruse. Sir Colin Halkett sent back to the rear the colours of his disorganised brigade. Further away, Cumberland's hussars turned tail, led by their colonel.

Outwardly calm, Wellington despatched several letters that would one day be published, including one to Ostend. He

Prince William of Prussia, 1797–1888, commander of the cavalry reserves of the 4th Prussian Corps. He was to become William I, Emperor of Germany.

could no longer hold out . . . the fleet would have to be warned . . . prepare to embark the army.

But to those around him he repeated: "Stand steadfast to the last." Then he looked first to the east and then to the west . . . for the Prussians or nightfall . . .

The 1st Prussian Corps was not far away. At Ohain its commander, Ziethen, was perplexed in the face of the retreats

Lieutenant-General Mouton, Count of Lobau, 1770–1838, commander of the 6th Corps. Lithograph by Delpech, after Maurin. Musée Royal de l'Armée, Brussels.

Lieutenant-General Count Duhesme, 1766–1815, commander-in-chief of the Imperial Young Guard. Lithograph by Paul Petit, after Llanta. Musée Royal de l'Armée, Brussels.

Plancenoit. View from the Charleroi road towards the height of Rossomme.

General von Sidow, commander of a reserve cavalry brigade of the 4th Prussian Corps. Bibliothèque Nationale, Paris.

Brigadier-General Pelet, 1779–1853, commander of the 2nd Regiment of Chasseurs à Pied of the Old Guard. Private collection.

and confusions that he could glimpse in the British ranks, particularly as several staff officers were signalling "The army is in difficulty".

At this moment Colonel Heymès, coming on behalf of Marshal Ney, was asking the Emperor for "a few infantry to finish them off".

"Where does he think I can find them?"

Napoleon had behind him only nine battalions of the Guard formed in square on both sides of the road, one battery and the duty squadron.

Should he leave Lobau, Duhesme and Pelet to deal as best they could with the Prussians that Grouchy should be attacking in the Limal direction and, with all that was to be found on the plain grouped around the Guard, march right over the British?

An immediate decision was essential since "victory is only a trollop!": because, down below, Ziethen was deploying his cavalry towards Ohain; because, at Plancenoit, Pirch I was preparing the removal of Lobau with 47 squadrons, 18 battalions and 100 guns . . .

And because Captain de Barail of the 2nd Carabiniers had just gone over to the lines of the British 52nd Regiment of Foot and was saying to Lieutenant-Colonel John Colborne and Major Fraser: "Napoleon is going to attack you with the Imperial Guard" – top-priority information given by a traitor, from which Wellington was to immediately profit. Two of Chassé's divisions and two of Brunswick's battalions were mustered in the centre. The artillery was ordered to cease firing and load with grape. Five fresh batteries were brought up to the front line. Maitland and Adam were ordered to move forward a little and have their men lie down among the crops in four ranks in a manner that would enable them to fire obliquely on their assailants. And Colin Halkett was ordered to station two regiments to the left of the Guards.

While breakfasting at Le Caillou that morning, the Emperor had said: "I will bring my artillery into play, I will order my cavalry to charge, and I will march with my Old Guard."

The sun broke through above Braine-l'Alleud.

Death of General Duhesme. Gravely wounded between Plancenoit and Rossomme, he was carried to the Roi d'Espagne inn at Genappe, where he was taken prisoner. Blücher came to visit him and had him cared for by the surgeon of his general staff. He died during the night of 19th to 20th June. Musée de l'Armée, Paris.

Right: *defence of the Plancenoit cemetery. Drawing by Victor Huen.*

The Prussian infantry attack at Plancenoit. Picture by Rochlling.

From 7 p.m. to 9 p.m.

The Guard attacks

Between 7.15 and 7.30 p.m. the last act of the drama was about to begin.

There were twelve battalions of the Middle Guard and Old Guard that Drouet had ordered to be drawn up in squares, 500 paces from each other, on both sides of the Brussels road, between La Belle-Alliance and the Decoster house. The 1st Battalion of the 1st Cuirassiers was left at Le Caillou. The 2nd Battalion of the 1st Grenadiers was guarding the Plan-

At Plancenoit, General Pelet tries to rally the infantry of the Young Guard while the 1st Battalion of the 2nd Regiment of the Chasseurs à Pied of the Old Guard comes up. By J. Girbal, from Soldats et Uniformes du 1er Empire.

cenoit road at "la Maison du Roi" in order to repel the Prussian spearheads. Level with it but on the other side of the road was the 1st Battalion of the regiment under General Petit, two hundred marines and sappers, and one battery remaining as a last reserve.

Reille regrouped his infantry to the south-east of Hougoumont. Ney sent d'Erlon once again towards the plateau and rallied the cuirassiers and the cavalry of the Guard. La Bédoyère and Gourgaud galloped up to announce that Grouchy would soon arrive to revive the morale of the troops, who had been disheartened by the set-backs and losses.

But Grouchy did not come. In the direction of Wavre, Pajol's and Vallin's artillery exchanged fire with that of Stülpnagel, the 31st Prussians and Kurmark's Landwehr on the Rixensart plateau.

There was no news of the patrols sent out towards Chapelle-Saint-Lambert.

In the distance, the sun was going down. Time was pressing. Bülow's cannonballs were now reaching the road. Ziethen's artillery went into action towards Ohain.

The large battery fired to its utmost.

Drums beating, the Guard marched off with the Emperor leading. The band of the Grenadiers played Gebauer's "La marche des bonnets à poil".

They were making for the British right centre – that is, between what is now the Butte du Lion and the crossroads.

The first six battalions – less than 3,000 men – advanced in lines of columns to the west of the road. These were the regiments of the Middle Guard 3rd and 4th Chasseurs and 3rd and 4th Grenadiers. Two horse-drawn guns of the Guard descended the slope in each space between two battalions. Baron Duchard, major of the horse artillery, was in command.

Three battalions of the Old Guard, 1,500 men, and the 2nd Battalion of the 1st and 2nd Chasseurs and of the 2nd Grenadiers followed in the second line. General Cambronne, adjutant of the 1st Chasseurs, General Roguet, second-in-command of the Grenadiers, and General Christiani, adjutant of the 2nd Grenadiers, rode at the head of their units.

Confronted by the Guard, the fugitives stopped in their tracks.

The Guard dealt with them.

The defence of La Haye-Sainte by the King's German Legion. To the right, the riflemen of the 95th attempt to put out the fire in one of the buildings. In the centre, the garrison prepares to carry out a bayonet charge. At 6 p.m. Marshal Ney, at the head of the 13th Light and a detachment of the 1st Engineers, took the farm while Major Baring and 42 survivors succeeded in piercing their assailants' front and regaining the British lines. By A. Northern. Landesgalerie, Hannover.

Lieutenant-General Count Morand, colonel-in-chief of the Chasseurs à Pied of the Old Guard. Musée de l'Armée, Paris.

At the sight of the dark greatcoats that forewarned of the passage of the legendary silhouette, the wounded sat up again; and the dispersed, the pursued and the desperate rallied to their battalions, their leaders, their colours.

Through the tangle of dead horses, twisted corpses and broken weapons, the phalanx reached the bottom of the valley.

Ney was to lead the attack with five battalions. The Emperor would himself station the sixth (the 2nd Battalion of the 3rd Grenadiers, under Belcourt) between Hougoumont and La Haye-Sainte, on the rising ground.

8 p.m. What remained of the Imperial army was ready for the final attack.

Smoke obscured the fading daylight.

The scanty battalions of the Middle Guard climbed the slopes of the plateau, the right flank forward; behind them came the three battalions of the Old Guard, then the Line, with the cavalry following, ready to exploit the issue. Everywhere could be heard drums beating the charge . . .

As if they sensed that they were about to die, the courageous men shouted "Long live the Emperor!"

At 6 p.m. the Prince of Orange, wounded, leaves the battlefield. After a painting by J. Odeware, detail.

The Papelotte farm in ruins. This was the bulwark of the British left flank. It was defended by the Nassau troops of Saxe-Weimar's brigade and was the scene of fierce fighting. Occupied by Durutte's division at about 7 p.m., it was retaken shortly afterwards by the Prussians. Watercolour by an unknown artist.

For fear of hitting the infantry, the guns of the main battery fell silent.

And those of the British artillery opened up. Fifty guns crashed out, double-charged and with canister. The weakened battalions of Kruse and the remainder of those of Ompteda, Kielmansegge and Brunswick dug in behind a chaotic barricade of discarded vehicles and ramparts of dead men. Chassé linked his battalions on the opposite slope.

In all, 50,000 men were awaiting 15,000, of which 6,500 were of the Guard. It was merely a question of the latter besting the former. Was that all? Well, they had so often been the bedfellows of Victory . . .

Coming out from the dead angle, without so much as a skirmisher to reconnoitre first, the grenadiers of the Middle Guard were taken to account by the artillery; but they closed ranks and overthrew two of Brunswick's battalions and two of Halkett's. Wounded in the hand, Friant withdrew, calling out "All goes well" when passing near the Old Guard, of which the Emperor directed the three battalions fundamentally from La Haye-Sainte.

But almost immediately Chassé unmasked a battery and threw forward six of Detmer's battalions, which flung the French back beyond the slope – where they were picked up by Cambronne's Chasseurs à Pied.

To the left, the 3rd and 4th Chasseurs advanced amid the wreckage, preceded by the generals on foot. At a point near the present Butte du Lion, a shouted order of "Stand up, Guards!" brought Maitland's men to their feet at thirty paces; and the order "Fire!" laid low Michel, Cardinal, Angelet, 20 officers and 400 men. The remainder, under cover provided by Belcourt's battalion, retreated to Hougoumont.

The attack by the Middle Guard lasted less than twenty minutes.

Sixty officers and 1,200 men had fallen; the rest had retreated; d'Erlon's line had ceded. The infantry under Bachelu, Foy and Pégot, sent into battle in front of La Haye-Sainte, having spread panic among Colin Halkett's division – certain officers of which cried with shame – fell back before the rifles of the 95th. The cavalry wheeled in a half-circle.

The three battalions of the Old Guard tried to cover the retreat: but they were soon submerged, and they fought on only for the honour of the regiment. The duty squadrons charged but were brought up sharply by Vivian's squadrons, which clattered down the slopes.

At the gallop on Copenhagen, Wellington, waving his hat, urged on some of his diminishing units.

Lieutenant-General Desvaux De Saint-Maurice, commander-in-chief of the artillery of the Guard. He was cut in two by a cannonball while at Napoleon's side. Collection of Commandant Lachouque.

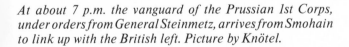

At about 7 p.m. the vanguard of the Prussian 1st Corps, under orders from General Steinmetz, arrives from Smohain to link up with the British left. Picture by Knötel.

Under the crossfire, to the "Hurrah!" of the British and the "Vorwärts!" of the Prussians came the answering French "Sauve qui peut" and dismal cries like the "It is the will of the gods" that had frozen ancient Rome with terror.

The same words will re-echo when the world comes to an end.

Preceding Wellington by two hundred metres, Napoleon remounted and made his way towards La Belle-Alliance. Ney, tattered, mad with rage, shouted to the square of the 95th, which was making an orderly retreat with its colour, "Come and see how a marshal of France dies" – but without managing to get himself killed. A howling mob drove back the fugitives.

Uhlans and Brandenburg dragoons were behind the 1st Silesian Hussars; Röder's cavalry was chasing what was left of d'Erlon's men. The French cannons were silent, overwhelmed. The Scots turned the guns against the infantry of Lobau, the Young Guard . . . Bülow's Prussians!

9 p.m. The moon shone spasmodically, fitfully illuminating some fantastic scenes. In burning Plancenoit, shooting was going on at point-blank range in the church and the cemetery. Pirch's Pomeranians were launched in successive waves in the midst of the flames, and the Young Guard of Duhesme were grievously hit. Pelet's veterans, overrun by Steinmetz, were bruised by 50 guns and surged back to the road. The 10th

of the Line – which the previous day had still been the Colonel-General regiment under General de Tromelin, the old émigré – was the last to retreat, in the name of military honour.

On the extreme right, Duuring's chasseurs were grappling with the 23rd Prussian Regiment.

The stable-lads harnessed the Imperial carriages.

What was to be done in the face of this rout – this onslaught launched over an area measuring half a league and lasting three-quarters of an hour?

Nothing. It was all over. The fall of Napoleon; the ruin of France; the British victory; the vengeance of Blücher; the triumph of the old Europe over the new . . . It was the end of an era.

On the feelings of all concerned, everything possible has already been written. These men, unleashed from the battle-field – intoxicated with fright, rage, joy, blood – expressed this fragment of history in cries of happiness, in oaths and curses that stirred the victors and consoled the vanquished. And perhaps the synthesis of all the shouting that went on during the evening of 18th June might well be the oath inaccurately attributed by posterity to Cambronne – "Merde!"

After 9 p.m.

Grenadier à Pied of the Old Guard in 1815. Lithograph by Raffet. Musée de l'Armée, Paris.

9 p.m. Where was the Emperor? Somewhere in the throng. They searched for him.

The battalions of the Guard that had just gone into action were no more. In their meagre squares of 50 metres a side, they had gathered a few of the fugitives and fired a few volleys at the British; and then, outflanked, cut down by sword and musket-shot, admitting it or not, they beat a retreat. The 2nd Battalion of the 2nd Grenadiers broke at the outset. The two battalions of the 3rd Chasseurs contained the British until nightfall and then dispersed and followed the torrent. The survivors of the only battalion of the 4th Chasseurs, having lost their commander and sixteen officers, joined up with the 3rd after a bloody clash near Hougoumont. The 2nd Battalion of the 2nd Chasseurs (under Mompez), supported by a few troops of cavalry, defended themselves, beat an orderly retreat and stopped at La Belle-Alliance. Then, reduced to about thirty men, it is probable that the last of the Old Guard dispersed.

For that part of it under Cambronne – the 2nd Battalion of the 1st Chasseurs – had already disappeared. Sent to the left by General Morand, it had clashed with the soldiers of Adam and Halkett. After a murderous conflict, it had repelled a charge by the 10th Hussars and had arrived at La Belle-Alliance much reduced in number. A few metres from Jérôme's Eagle, Cambronne was hit in the head by a cannon-ball and collapsed. The battalion then dispersed. The 1st Battalion of the 3rd Grenadiers was decimated by artillery

The Emperor at the head of the battalions of the Middle Guard, which he was to lead to the place of the attack. By Jean Augé, from Champs de Bataille de Waterloo, *L. Garros.*

Lieutenant-General Count Drouot, 1774-1847, deputy chief of staff in command of the Imperial Guard. Bulloz.

fire; and the only battalion of the 4th Grenadiers was almost entirely wiped out. A few survivors carried off and saved their leader, the adjutant, Harlet: and "père Roguet" went off with Belcourt's battalion (the 2nd of the 3rd Grenadiers), posted as advanced sentries by the Emperor. The glory that had attached itself to his retreat had spread over the whole corps. Attacked to the north of Hougoumont by the British

Lieutenant-General Count Friant, commander-in-chief of the Grenadiers à Pied of the Imperial Guard. Collection of Commandant Lachouque.

Brigadier-General Christiani, commander of the 2nd Regiment of Grenadiers à Pied of the Old Imperial Guard. Musée des Arts Décoratifs.

Attack of the Imperial Guard. By Woodville. Musée de l'Armée, Paris.

187

Attack of the Middle Guard. The squares of the 3rd Chasseurs à Pied. Picture by Jean Augé.

Wellington gives the order to Maitland's guards to open fire on the 1st and 2nd Battalions of the 3rd Chasseurs. Sketch by Captain Jones, from The Battle of Waterloo, 1817.

The British Army descends to the plateau of Mont-Saint-Jean.

General Chassé leads the Dutch-Belgian counter-attack by Detmers' brigade, which is coming down the slopes of Mont-Saint-Jean with bayonets ready. Drawing by James Thiriar. Musée Royal de l'Armée, Brussels.

cavalry under Vandeleur, the square was surrounded and decimated – reduced, little by little, to a meagre triangle. Firing a final volley, to shouts of "Long live the Emperor!", it then split up into small groups that managed to reach Rossomme...

Near the farm, the drums of the 1st Grenadiers beat the "Grenadiers" and the "Carabinière" to call stray grenadiers and chasseurs, who gradually filled to the brim their squares that were already crammed with soldiers and generals: Petit, Soult, Bertrand, Drouot, Flahaut, La Bédoyère, Ney, the Emperor. Tears streamed from their eyes.

It was about 9.30 p.m.

General advance by the British Army. After a painting by Granville Baker.

Colonel Colbourne, commanding officer of the 52nd Light Infantry Regiment.

The 52nd Light Infantry captures a French battery

House of the guide Decoster, near which the two battalions of the 1st Grenadiers formed in square.

Square of the 4th Grenadiers. Collection of Viscount Henri de Beaufort.

Napoleon at the centre of the square of the 1st Battalion of the 1st Regiment of Grenadiers of the Guard.

The rout

At 9.30 p.m. General Gourguad gives the order for the firing of the last rounds of the French cannon in the battle. Collection of Commandant Lachouque.

The vice clamped down on the Grande Armée. On foot, on horseback, the men fled southwards. Who was that on the right? On the left . . . ? Friend or foe? Dörnberg's squadrons, pushed back towards Hougoumont by the French cuirassiers, ran into groups under the command of Foy and Bachelu and cut down, by error, some companies of the 95th British – who were firing into the pack . . . Chassé's battalions were halted by a volley of shot coming from the west . . . And those troopers shouting? Were they hussars? The 10th? Vandeleur's light dragoons, in pursuit of Piré's lancers, were broken by a fusillade. The Imperial Guard? No. It was Hanoverians who had lost their way . . .

There was confusion everywhere. Cannonballs from three countries fell at random. The last 12-pounder battery of the Guard had just been silenced 150 metres to the right. It had fired its last rounds; then the charge went off – and Lord Uxbridge, the commander, lost a leg.

On the road, the grenadiers fired a volley . . . they had seen hussars. British? Prussian? French?

The Emperor tried to stop the fugitives, perhaps in the hope of being killed.

The rout. By Jo[...]

192

He would have to depart if he wanted to evade capture, for everything ahead of him was in enemy hands.

Napoleon therefore gave Petit the order to retreat, abandoning to the enemy 250 guns and 400 vehicles.

A throng of men, horses and waggons was fleeing towards the south, obstructing the road that climbed to Le Caillou. The Emperor's square had difficulty in reaching the orchard. They cleared the way with blows from the flat of their swords. Most of the vehicles had left for Genappe, where nothing had been organised or even planned to ensure the crossing of the Dyle. The only available carriages belonged to the Emperor and his 'household'. With time pressing, Napoleon forsook his mare La Désirée, mounted a troop horse presented to him by his page Gudin and reached the road leading to Charleroi, followed by Duuring's chasseurs. Behind him, the 1st Grenadiers, the lancers and the chasseurs of the Guard protected him, halting now and then to deploy and fire – "Ready", as one of them wrote later, "to be hacked to death in order to defend him from those savage Prussians, Röder's dragoons and the uhlans and hussars of Prince William."

At La Belle-Alliance, Wellington ordered his cavalry – "tired to death" – to halt, leaving it to Blücher to take care of pursuing the enemy. The two commanders embraced and congratulated each other while the bands played the "Pariser Einzugs Marsch" and "God Save the King", Lulli's hymn that was sung for the first time at Saint-Cyr by Madame de Maintenon's young ladies on the occasion of a visit by Louis XIV.

Brigadier-General Count Cambronne, 1770–1842, commander of the 1st Regiment of Chasseurs à Pied of the Old Guard. Bulloz.

General Baron Gourgaud, 1783–1852, an officer of the Emperor's personal staff. Lithograph by Formentin. Musée Royal de l'Armée, Brussels.

Marshal Ney addressing the 95th Infantry (Brue's brigade), which fell back in good order around its Eagle. "Come and see how a marshal of France dies." Painting by E. Chaperon.

The last square.

Meanwhile, in blazing Plancenoit, the infantry, shakos on the end of their muskets, chanted Luther's old hymn (music by Niceitas) that the soldiers of Frederick II had sung at Leuthen on 5th December 1757: "Herr Gott, wir loben Dich; Herr Gott wir danken Dir . . . " ("God, we praise You; God, we thank You . . . ").

Old Vorwärts gave his orders for the pursuit of the French "so long as there is one man and one horse still standing". Bülow and Ziethen were to go towards Genappe. Pirch was to go towards Mansart to cut off Grouchy's retreat.

At this moment Grouchy was at Bierges and at Wavre on the Dyle. His troops were bivouacking within reach of the infantry of the 3rd Prussian Corps, installed in the Rixensart woods. At daybreak he intended to throw the Prussians back to Louvain and then go on to Brussels to rejoin the Emperor, who must certainly be heading towards that city close on the heels of Wellington through the forest of Soignes.

Alone, followed at a distance by five officers, Wellington set off from La Belle-Alliance in the direction of Waterloo and traversed the field of carnage and terror – so often described since – dominated by the constant dismal cries of those who were dying without succour or sacrament.

The balance sheet was indeed dramatic: out of 73,900 men present at the beginning of the battle, the Imperial Army had lost 36 generals, 720 officers and 24,000 men killed or wounded. The Army of the Low Countries professed a loss of 15,000 men out of the 67,000 engaged. The 48,000 Prussians who had come in towards the end of the battle lost 6,000 between them. Some regiments were particularly hard-hit: the battalion of the British 27th Regiment of Foot (678 men) left 478 at the crossroads of Mont-Saint-Jean; the 18th Prussians, about 2,000 strong engaged at Plancenoit, lost 800. All of the officers of the 4th Grenadiers, the 4th Chasseurs and the 3rd Chasseurs of the Imperial Guard had been killed or wounded but for one or two.

10.30 p.m. Back in his room, Wellington began to draft his report to Lord Bathurst:

. . . Napoleon having collected from the 10th to the 14th of this month the 1st, 2nd, 3rd, 4th and 6th corps, as well as the Imperial Guards and nearly all the cavalry on the Sambre . . .

I have the satisfaction of assuring your Lordship that the army never conducted itself better on any occasion . . .

At Brussels, horsemen arrived shouting "Victory!". Lights appeared all over the town. After the earlier anxiety, caused by fugitives shouting "Every man for himself!", there was an outburst of joy.

At Ghent, Louis XVIII was conferring with Blacas, Richelieu, Clarke and the two Imperial marshals Marmont and Victor. The waggon of the crown diamonds was harnessed.

Chateaubriand, who heard the gunfire while standing at the foot of a poplar tree, meditated anxiously. "Lawfulness should return behind these men in red who have just redyed their crimson in the blood of the French," he wrote.

At 1 a.m. a letter from Pozzo di Borgo announced that Bonaparte had lost "the battle of Waterloo".

A Prussian detachment, commanded by Major Keller, seizes Napoleon's carriage.

"The guard dies but does not surrender." By Job.

The pursuit. In the centre, escorted by Lützow's lancers, a Prussian infantry drummer is mounted on one of the horses of the Emperor's retinue. To the left, French prisoners. By Knötel.

Meeting of Wellington and Blücher at about 9.30 p.m. at La Belle-Alliance. By Knötel.

Napoleon approached Quatre-Bras. Astride his badly trained and nervy troop horse he proceeded amid his chasseurs, accompanied by Soult, Bertrand, Drouot, La Bédoyère and Gudin. He spoke little . . . Officers and soldiers emerged from their own thoughts only to observe him "sombre, impassive, probing the future and seeing the collapse . . ." Some of the chasseurs heard him say, "After today, there is nothing more . . . nothing . . . but I must go to Paris." Then he asked for news of Ney and Grouchy.

At Genappe, in the confusion and the mob that Provost Marshal General Radet was trying to straighten out at his peril, Napoleon was nearly captured. He was forced to abandon his coach to Major Keller and the fusiliers of the 15th Prussian Regiment, who went off with his personal belongings. And with them went the proclamations to the Belgians and to the inhabitants on the left bank of the Rhine:

The ephemeral success of my enemies has separated you for a moment from my Empire. In my exile, I heard your pleas . . . The God of War has decided the destiny of your beautiful provinces. Napoleon is among you. Rally to my invincible ranks . . .

At 10 p.m. Wellington drafts his Waterloo despatch. In the next room Colonel Gordon, his aide-de-camp, is dying. After a portrait by Lady Burghersh.

At Quatre-Bras there were appalling scenes . . . Over an area no bigger than the field of Mars, 800 horses and 4,000 men awaited burial. Around the outskirts of the Bossu woods, Dutch, Scottish and French spectres – hussars of Death – grimaced under the flames of several fires.

In the middle of the crossroads, arms crossed, a tragic figure in his grey frock-coat, Napoleon stared fixedly towards Waterloo.

Some of the fugitive soldiers recognised him, stepped aside and then moved on. In the distance could be heard the Pomeranian drum, the thin sound of which pursued the French.

"Who are you?"

"The lancers of your Guard, sire," answered Colbert.

"Ah! Yes . . . Where is Piré?"

Silence. Piré was in command of the 2nd Cavalry Division, which had not been engaged in the battle.

"We do not know, sire."

"What? And the 6th Lancers?"

"They weren't with us."

That fixed stare.

"But who are you, then?"

"Sire, I am Colbert and these are the Lancers of your Guard."

"Ah! Yes . . . and the 6th Lancers? And Piré? Piré!"

Depression? Agitation? Bewilderment?

It was time to move on . . . to warn Grouchy . . . to send him the order to withdraw to Namur, Givet, France . . .

Captain Demonceau, aide-de-camp to General Gressot, Deputy Chief of Staff, was selected for the task . . . He went off alone, in the middle of the night, on a tired horse. His course was a distance of thirty or forty kilometres, perhaps more, over countryside he did not know, infested with enemies . . .

However, the lives of 32,000 men were at stake. So everyone had lost his head.

The Emperor put his foot in the stirrup and dropped heavily into the saddle.

The riders moved off towards Charleroi.

Napoleon reached Philippeville and then Laon, which he left at 9 p.m. on the 20th to arrive in Paris on the morning of the 21st.

General Count Pajol, 1772–1844, commander of the 1st Cavalry Corps.

Lieutenant-General Teste, commander of the 21st Infantry Division which, as rear-guard, stopped the Prussians at the gates of Namur, allowing the rest of the army corps to fall back to the frontier.

The 20th Regiment of Dragoons, General Exelmans' corps. In reserve on 20th June. Drawing by James Thiriar.

The Bridge of Christ, at Wavre. Engraving by Sturm.

197

Epilogue

The day after the battle. Radio Times Hulton Picture Library.

A convoy of guns captured from the French goes through the village of Waterloo on 19th June, passing Wellington's headquarters.

On the Dyle, 19th June began with a Prussian attack that failed. Thielmann, forced to retreat, could have fallen back on Brussels – which would have been especially logical since he had learned at 9 o'clock of the victory at Waterloo. But the previous day Blücher had told him, on leaving, "In the event of a set-back, retreat to Louvain." Therefore, having encountered a set-back at Wavre, Thielmann fell back to Louvain. Relentless reasoning, but absurd.

And Grouchy, who still did not know the outcome of the battle, was going to march on Brussels! His right flank was at Bawette. He ordered a few squadrons to pursue the Prussians.

10.30 p.m. A rider arrived – hatless, jacket and trousers torn, dirty, a three-day growth of beard, his horse trembling on its legs.

It was Demonceau. And he stammered out alarming utterances incoherently: rout . . . the Emperor . . . the dead . . . the Guard . . . the Emperor!

There was nothing more to be drawn out of him. Was he drunk? Mad? Demonceau had no written orders. Had he received any? No one knew.

Gradually – calmed, tended, fed – the officer recovered his self-control and announced the defeat, describing the rout of the army . . . the Emperor at Quatre-Bras . . . It was now 1 a.m. . . .

The marshal must withdraw towards the Sambre, Namur, France.

Grouchy's situation was critical. He was alone with his small detachment behind enemy armies which could, and would, cut him off from all retreat and annihilate his forces. It would be child's play for Blücher and Wellington.

The marshal immediately issued his orders.

Under the protection of Pajol's cavalry, which would maintain contact with the Prussians, the detachment would set off in two columns towards Namur: that on the right (4th Corps and convoy) would go by way of Gembloux; that on the left (3rd Corps) would go by way of Grand-Leez. One cavalry division would cover the right flank. Exelmans' dragoons would overtake the columns and occupy the Namur bridges as soon as possible.

By the grace of God!

Without that, Grouchy would be lost. He had on his right flank two armies less the Prussian 3rd Corps, which was behind him.

This is what happened.

Pirch I (2nd Corps), whose troops had not been engaged in the Waterloo battle, received at 11 p.m. on the 18th the order to cut off Grouchy's retreat. He did not arrive at Millery (17 kilometres away) until 11 a.m. on the 19th, and he rested there until 5 a.m. on the 20th.

General von Thielmann (3rd Corps) noticed too late that the French had gone and did not set off in pursuit until the morning of the 20th.

By then, Grouchy was far away.

One brigade of dragoons had taken the bridges across the Sambre and the Meuse at 4 p.m. on the 20th; Exelmans' division was the first to cross at 7 p.m. The columns and covering units bivouacked on the line Mazy–Temploux–Rhisne. Grouchy gave his orders for the entry into Namur.

On the morning of the 20th, he was attacked by the vanguards of the Prussian 1st Corps and 3rd Corps. Foot by foot, the French 3rd Corps and Teste's division (6th Corps) resisted to enable the artillery, the convoys, the wounded, the 4th Corps and the cavalry to get through. At Namur, the gateway to Brussels was heroically defended in a bloody conflict. At 6 p.m., Marshal Grouchy's detachment being on the way to Givet – where it arrived on the evening of the 21st – Teste's division, reduced to 2,000 bayonets, withdrew without giving the alarm, crossed the barricaded bridges by filing along the parapets and reached Dinant through the Porte de France, which they set on fire.

"You have rendered a service to France that will be held in repute by the whole world," the Minister of War wrote to Marshal Grouchy on 23rd June.

On the previous day – Thursday, 22nd June – eight days after the crossing of the Sambre, Napoleon signed his second abdication . . . while the troops from Waterloo regrouped around Laon to march on Paris, followed at a distance by the British columns by way of Péronne and Blücher's troops by way of Guise.

Napoleon had lost the battle of Waterloo. The defeat could not be imputed to the delays or the "follies" of Ney, or to Grouchy's hesitations, or to the errors of Drouet d'Erlon, or to the slackness of Reille . . . all subordinates, acting under Imperial orders that had sent them off or recalled them in the normal manner.

The responsibility for defeat, as well as for victory, devolves upon the Commander-in-Chief.

Despite innumerable obstacles, he had forged an army from a mass of uncoordinated troops – from officers uncertain whether they should follow the "usurper" or the King, such as Bourmont and several others who deserted while, on the heights of Charleroi, the soldiers spat out their disgust for the disloyal general and passionately acclaimed their Emperor as he sat astride a chair in front of the Belle-Vue tavern, drowsy and looking older.

Napoleon had appointed Grouchy as marshal and put him at the head of an army: Grouchy – one of the victors of Hohenlinden, a brilliant handler of cavalry at Friedland, at Borodino, and in Champagne during the previous year – the man who had just annihilated the Duke of Angoulême but had never before held supreme command. He had entrusted to Ney two army corps despite his repudiations and the dreadful abdication scene at Fontainebleau. He had summoned to his side Soult, who had betrayed the Empire and had in turn been the ardent apologist of the King and then the outright detractor of the Bourbons; the man who had been ambitious for the Portuguese crown after threatening it with a firing squad.

And before leaving Paris, he had not had Fouché executed. Napoleon believed that his enemies were second-rate and that his authority and prestige would suppress his opponents. However, if on the battlefield military honour imposed silence on politics, the men and the Emperor himself had changed.

"The loss of time is irreparable in war," Napoleon had written to his brother Joseph on 20th March 1806. "The reasons that one pleads are always bad since operations do not lack delays." And on the 15th, sleeping at Belle-Vue, he had lost five hours – during which Ziethen's Prussians had escaped. On the night of the 16th/17th he had lost fifteen hours: instead of pursuing Blücher's defeated army to the death, he had allowed it to fall back on Wavre and found it confronting him again on the 18th at Waterloo.

In the early hours of the 17th he could, in accordance with his "way", have held Wellington's Anglo-Netherlanders in a pincer movement between the guns of d'Erlon, Ney, Lobau, the Guard, and two cavalry divisions – all of which were covered by Grouchy; he could have thrown them back far from Genappe and marched on Brussels – without the Prussians, who were entangled in the depths of Mont-Saint-Jean, being able to intervene. But he had tarried at Fleurus, visited

Prix: 15 fr. pour trois mois, 29 fr. pour six mois, 56 pour l'année. (Les lettres doivent être affranchies.)

(N°. 185.)

S'adresser pour les abonnemens à la Feuille du Jour, rue Neuve..., N°. 45.

FEUILLE DU JOUR.

(MARDI 4 JUILLET AN 1815.)

NOUVELLES ÉTRANGÈRES.

ANGLETERRE.

Londres, 27 juin.

Le *Morning-Chronicle* et le *Statesman*, atterrés par la défaite et l'abdication de leur cher empereur Napoléon, se consolent en injuriant les Bourbons et en répandant tous les bruits qu'ils jugent les plus propres à desservir la cause de cette dynastie. Le *Statesman* a fabriqué des nouvelles de Paris d'après lesquelles on y aurait proclamé la république française, en donnant le commandement des armées au général Bonaparte, et en déclarant une guerre éternelle à tous les tyrans. Le *Morning-Chronicle* fait de graves remontrances au lord Castlereagh, sur le projet qu'il suppose à ce ministre de travailler au rétablissement du roi de France, et à l'extirpation totale du jacobinisme; ce journal se permet même de révoquer en doute une déclaration du duc d'Orléans, dans laquelle ce prince professe les principes admis par le droit public de l'Europe sur la légitimité des souverains, et annonce que l'extinction totale de la branche des Bourbons peut seule lui ouvrir l'accès du trône français. Le *Morning Chronicle* a même l'impudence d'affirmer que l'opinion personnelle du duc d'Orléans est que la volonté du peuple dispose légalement de la couronne.

— Les détails qu'on apprend sur la grande bataille du 18, sont aussi nombreux qu'intéressans. Le duc de Wellington, dans une lettre à sa mère, lady Mornington, parle avec admiration de l'activité et de l'habileté que Bonaparte a déployées dans cette sanglante journée. «Je n'exalte pas mon adversaire, ajoute-t-il, par un adroit calcul de vanité; car, ce n'est pas moi qui l'ai vaincu; la victoire est uniquement due à la force physique et à la constance inébranlable des troupes anglaises.» Le champ de bataille offrit un spectacle sans pareil; les débris de canons et de caissons, les tas d'hommes et de chevaux morts couvraient une vaste étendue. L'horreur qu'inspirait cette scène n'a pas refroidi l'humanité des habitants de Bruxelles; beaucoup d'individus des deux sexes ont accouru sur le champ de bataille et ont prodigué des soins aux blessés. On cite divers traits de cette grande journée. Le général Picton a trouvé la mort en essayant d'enfoncer à la baïonnette, à la tête de son infanterie, un carré de cavalerie française, manœuvre qui lui avait réussi en Espagne. Son corps a été retrouvé dans un champ nouvellement labouré; il était percé de trois coups de lance; son cheval, épuisé de fatigues, se tenait debout auprès de son maître.

Le prince d'Orange avait été un moment au pouvoir de l'ennemi; dégagé par le septième bataillon belge, il jeta au milieu de ces braves ses décorations en s'écriant: c'est vous qui avez tous ensemble mérité cet ordre! les officiers suspendirent ces marques d'honneurs au drapeau de leur corps. Les troupes de Brunswick ont fait des prodiges de valeur pour venger la mort de leur souverain. Déjà en partant de leur pays, elles avaient, par ordre de ce prince, mis un crêpe autour de leur drapeau, en signe de deuil, pour feu le duc de Brunswick, connu par la campagne de 1792 et dont quelques Français, émissaires de Bonaparte, ont violé le tombeau. Le 1er. et le 3e. corps d'armée français avaient, de leur côté, arboré le drapeau noir, pour indiquer qu'ils ne feraient point de prisonniers.

L'histoire de la guerre moderne n'offre aucun exemple de la fureur avec laquelle les Français attaquèrent cinq fois de suite, ni de la constance avec laquelle les alliés les repoussèrent. Il est faux que les alliés aient eu la supériorité du nombre: l'armée de Wellington, présente sur le champ de bataille, était de 64 mille hommes, et celle de Blücher de 50 mille; les Français étaient au nombre de 120 mille hommes.

La ferme nommée la *Belle-Alliance* ayant été le centre de l'action, la station de Bonaparte et le lieu où Wellington et Blücher se virent sur la fin du combat, ces deux généraux ont décidé qu'il fallait profiter de l'allusion heureuse que présente ce nom, en désignant la journée sous celui de *Bataille de la Belle-Alliance*.

La déroute de l'armée française lui a été d'autant plus funeste, que les Prussiens l'ont poursuivie sans relâche toute la nuit du 18 au 19, et le jour suivant. Le maréchal Blücher criait lui-même à ses soldats : « Mes enfants, poursuivons-les ce soir, afin qu'il n'en revienne pas un demain matin. » C'est le général Ziethen qui a dirigé la poursuite. Dans les voitures de Bonaparte qui ont été prises, on a trouvé sa décoration de l'aigle noir de Prusse, qui a pour légende : *suum cuique* (à chacun son bien); on y a aussi trouvé un grand nombre de proclamations révolutionnaires, datées d'avance du palais de Laeken, adressées aux Belges; elles n'auraient pas produit grand effet, car le peuple à Bruxelles est furieux contre les Français, et a même voulu maltraiter les prisonniers de guerre.

Bonaparte fit une tentative pour arrêter le torrent des fuyards, il plaça au pont de Charleroy un bataillon; la baïonnette au bout du fusil; mais ce bataillon fut renversé en un instant. Bonaparte portait sa redingote grise et un chapeau rond.

— Lorsque Regnault (de Saint-Jean d'Angély), comme organe du conseil des ministres, eut déclaré à Bonaparte que l'intérêt de la France exigeait son abdication : « Comment! que dites-vous? » s'écria Bonaparte; et, *toi aussi Brutus!* » Le *Morning-Chronicle* ne dit pas si, à ce mot, M. Regnault (de Saint-Jean-d'Angély) se couvrit le visage de son manteau.

— Il a circulé à Londres une adresse au peuple français par le duc d'Orléans. Le *Morning-Chronicle* dit qu'il est autorisé à déclarer que c'est une pièce fausse.

BELGIQUE.

Bruxelles, 23 juin.

La reddition de Maubeuge paraît certaine. On assure que Louis XVIII quitte Gand aujourd'hui pour aller fixer provisoirement le siège de son gouvernement à Maubeuge.

— Une division française de huit mille hommes, qui était restée près de Wavres, en est partie avant-hier à cinq heures du matin pour retourner en France. Elle a été poursuivie sans relâche par les troupes prussiennes. Plusieurs affaires sanglantes ont eu lieu, dans lesquelles les Français ont eu cinq mille hommes tués, blessés ou prisonniers; les autres trois mille hommes se sont échappés en gagnant la Meuse, qu'ils ont traversée entre Namur et Dinant.

— S. A. R. le prince d'Orange n'a pas passé une très bonne nuit. Néanmoins l'état de sa santé était fort satisfaisant ce matin. Le prince n'a pas de fièvre, et la blessure a la plus belle apparence.

— Le capitaine Burghagen a été témoin de la capture de la voiture de Napoléon; la portière était ouverte, comme si la voiture venait d'être abandonnée à l'instant. On a pris aussi d'autres voitures, dans lesquelles on a trouvé une grande quantité d'argent et d'or monnayé, outre l'argenterie et d'autres valeurs.

FRANCE.

Paris, 3 juillet.

Des négociations ont commencé aujourd'hui à 7 heures du matin, entre la commission de gouvernement et les généraux ennemis. Pendant toute la journée il a existé, de fait, une suspension d'armes entre les deux armées. On a vu des généraux français et ennemis traverser les lignes et se rendre aux quartiers généraux opposés; pendant ce temps-là, les soldats des avant-gardes fraternisaient et buvaient ensemble. Les négociations ont pris une tournure favorable, et l'on est déjà d'accord sur les points principaux...

Chelsea Pensioners reading the Waterloo despatch. Detail from a painting by Sir David Wilkie. Victoria and Albert Museum.

the battlefield in his coach, ridden to Ligny and Brye, comforted the wounded, entered into discussions with his generals about Jacobin politics and liberal and loyalist politics, playing the Emperor in the manner of Epinal – and it was only between 11 a.m. and noon that he had thought to send Lobau towards Marbais and Grouchy against the Prussians, whom he believed to be heading for Namur.

"It is a bad principle of war to follow the enemy on his own ground," he had often said. But he had followed Wellington to Mont-Saint-Jean and Blücher to Sombreffe.

"When you want to do battle, muster all your forces, not neglecting any of them; a battalion sometimes decides a battle," he was to explain to Montholon. But on the 18th, nine battalions had remained at Ligny and almost as many at Charleroi. Grouchy had sixty-two under his command. It is very unlikely, however, that Napoleon could have hoped for the marshal to arrive on the Waterloo battlefield since, at 10 a.m., he had sent him an order to march on Wavre. This

order was confirmed at 2 p.m., at the same time inviting Grouchy to "manoeuvre in the direction of Mont-Saint-Jean" – although Grouchy could not fight at Wavre and manoeuvre towards Mont-Saint-Jean at the same time.

The Emperor also knew that the bearers of these orders could not reach their destinations before 2.30 p.m. and 6 p.m. respectively and that the marshal's detachment would require – as would the Prussians – from six to eight hours to reach him.

This is why the Emperor stated that fate was no longer on his side. He said it to his companions in captivity . . .

I sensed that Fortune was abandoning me. I no longer had in me the feeling of final success. Not to venture is to do nothing when the moment is right, and one should never venture without being convinced of good luck.

Pilgrims to Waterloo, pause a while near La Belle-Alliance in front of the eagle with the broken wings at the spot where Napoleon saw his star disappear beyond the horizon. Look at the ridges of Mont-Saint-Jean, Hougoumont, the vale of La Haye-Sainte; contemplate in the presence of those who have been sleeping there since that day of mortal combat. You will realise that a European drama drew to a close there. The curtain fell on the last act, begun on 2nd June 1812, when the Army of Europe crossed the Niemen.

The Confederation of Free Europe, of Mediterranean civilisation, collapsed under the blows of the Old Europe of the Holy Alliance.

At St. Helena, Napoleon foresaw the consequences of this disaster.

Europe will be united or it will perish . . .

The agglomeration of Europe will come sooner or later, in the nature of things; the impetus has been given and I do not think that there can be in Europe any other stability than the agglomeration of the great nations . . .

For one hundred and sixty years statesmen have been endeavouring to rebuild that which Napoleon had constructed in fifteen years and which was destroyed in ten hours at Waterloo.

e Waterloo banquet, held on the anniversary of the battle. The Duke of Wellington presides, surrounded by the survivors of the celebrated campaign. Sir William Salter. Apsley House. Reproduced by gracious permission of H.M. the Queen.

The last tribute from the conqueror.

Painting by C. R. Leslie Apsley House.